W9-CPC-952

THE
ENCYCLOPEDIA
OF
Awesome Space

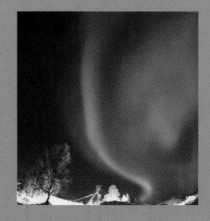

© Aladdin Books Ltd 2001
Produced by
Aladdin Books Ltd
28 Percy Street
London W1P 0LD

ISBN 0-7613-2276-0

First published in the United States in 2001 by
Copper Beech Books
2 Old New Milford Road
Brookfield,
Connecticut 06804

Designers:
Flick, Book design and graphics
Simon Morse

Editor:
Liz White

Consultant:
Robin Scagell

Illustrators:
Ian Thompson, Mike Saunders, Rob Shone,
Peter Kesteven, Graham White, Simon Tegg,
Colin Howard—SGA, Alex Pang, Richard Rockwood

Cartoons:
Jo Moore

Picture Research:
Brian Hunter Smart

Certain illustrations have appeared in earlier
books created by Aladdin Books.

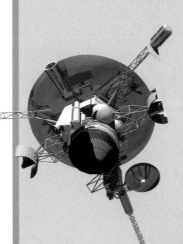

Cataloging-in-Publication Data is on file
at the Library of Congress.

THE
ENCYCLOPEDIA
— OF —
Awesome Space

John Farndon

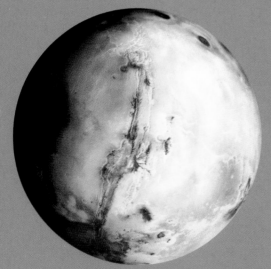

COPPER BEECH BOOKS
Brookfield, Connecticut

Contents

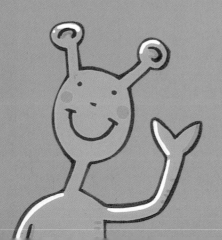

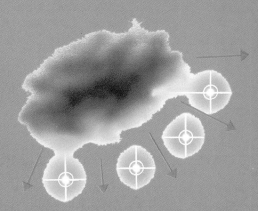

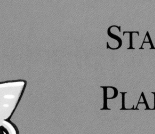

Introduction

Have you ever looked into the night sky and wondered what was out there?

There is a whole family of planets in our Solar System, but do you know what lies beyond?

This book will take you off into the Solar System to explore the planets and their moons. You will learn all about the Sun and the stars that light up the sky. Find out about how the Universe started and how it may end, and learn about the amazing journeys that astronauts have made into space.

• In this book, a billion is one thousand million.

Spot and count!

Q: Why watch for these boxes?

A: They give answers to the space questions you always wanted to ask.

zoom in on...

Space bits

Look for these boxes to take a closer look at space features.

Awesome factS

Look for these diamonds to learn more about the truly weird and wonderful facts about stars, the planets, the Universe, and space exploration!

Watch for the yellow bands at the top of the pages. They contain facts that are out of this world!

Chapter 1

The Sun and other stars

When you look into the sky on a clear night, you will see thousands of stars. You cannot see them in the daytime since the sky is too bright, but they are still there. The star groups do not change, which makes it easy to learn your way around.

You do not need any equipment to study the stars. With the naked eye alone you can see the Milky Way, watch for shooting stars, or pick out some of the main star groups.

Awesome facts
The stars are huge. The smallest star
is one hundred times larger than
Jupiter, the largest planet in
our Solar System.

Looking through binoculars, the
Milky Way becomes thousands
of individual stars. Some brighter
galaxies show up as fuzzy light.
You can see more clearly the
difference in color and
brightness of individual stars.

Looking with a telescope, you
can see even more detail. You
can see craters on the Moon, the
rings of Saturn, and clouds of
dust and gas like the Orion
nebula, just below Orion's belt,
where stars are being born.

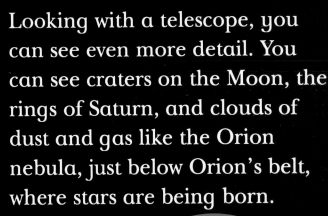

zoom in on...

Candle power

An area of the Sun's surface the size of a postage stamp shines with the power of one and a half million candles! This is why the Sun is bright enough to light up the Earth 93 million miles (150 million km) away.

Every now and then, huge, flamelike looping plumes of hot gas erupt from the Sun's surface (above). These plumes are called solar prominences.

10

Our amazing Sun

The Sun is a star, and like all stars it is a huge fiery ball. The temperature at the center of the Sun reaches over 27 million °F (15m °C)! The Sun is much hotter than any fire on Earth, and is hot enough to melt any known substance. Inside the Sun, one kind of gas is changing into another. This is what makes it shine.

Awesome factS

The Sun weighs 333,420 times more than the Earth and is 110 times wider. In fact, you could fit 1.3 million Earths into the Sun!

Q: What are sunspots?

A: Sunspots are dark patches on the Sun's surface. They look black because they are not as hot as the gas around them. The largest sunspots cover an area 150 times bigger than Earth.

The Sun

The Sun in the sky

The Sun gives off incredible amounts of heat and light in all directions. Only a tiny fraction hits the Earth, but it provides our planet with virtually all its energy. Without the Sun, the Earth would be almost pitch black all the time and colder than the coldest winter imaginable in the Arctic.

Sun's rays

Q: What are the auroras ?

A: Auroras are amazing glowing lights that can occur in the skies above the North and South Poles. They are created when streams of electrically charged particles from the Sun enter the Earth's atmosphere.

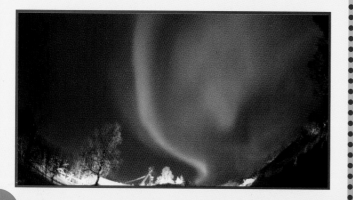

zoom in on...

Equator

The power of the Sun is strongest along the equator, the imaginary line around the middle of the Earth. This is because the equator is the closest point on the Earth to the Sun, so the Sun's rays have less distance to travel.

The Earth is surrounded by a magnetic field. This field protects the Earth from the solar wind, a stream of particles that flows from the Sun. When these particles do manage to enter the Earth's atmosphere, usually at the North and South Poles, they cause auroras.

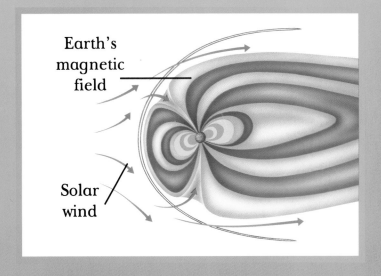

Earth's magnetic field

Solar wind

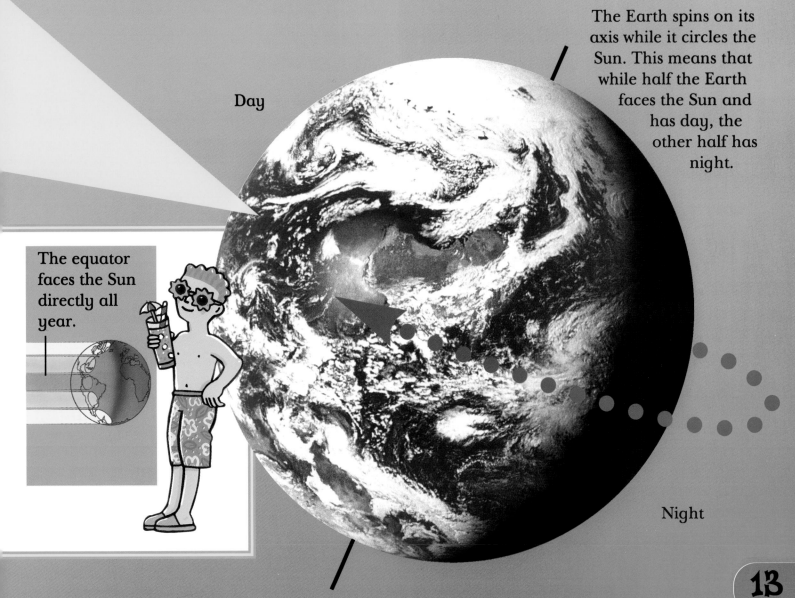

The Earth spins on its axis while it circles the Sun. This means that while half the Earth faces the Sun and has day, the other half has night.

Day

The equator faces the Sun directly all year.

Night

During a total eclipse of the Sun, the Moon passes exactly in front of the Sun. All that can be seen of the Sun is its corona—its halo of glowing gases. Sometimes, you may see more of the Sun glinting through a valley on the Moon, making it look like a wedding ring with a bright stone.

Total solar eclipse

Moon

Moon's orbit

Partial solar eclipse

Earth

Moon

Lunar eclipse

Awesome factS

Astronomers can predict to the exact second when an eclipse will happen. They can also predict them many years in advance.

Sun

Switching the Sun off

Amazingly, because the Sun is so far away, it looks the same size as the Moon in the sky—but it is actually 400 times bigger around! Every now and then, the Moon passes in front of the Sun and blocks it out so that a small area on Earth gets dark during the daytime. This is called a solar eclipse.

Once or twice in most years, the Moon goes around into the Earth's shadow. This is a lunar eclipse. You see the Earth's shadow as a dark disk creeping across the Moon's face for a few hours. Sometimes the Moon turns deep red.

zoom in on...

Chinese dragon swallows the Sun!

Some ancient Chinese believed that during a solar eclipse the Sun was being swallowed by a giant reptile. But Chinese scientists understood and recorded eclipses as astronomical events as long ago as 1360 BC.

Q: How do you find the Pole Star?

A: The Pole Star sits above the North Pole. You can find it by looking for the Big Dipper, a group of seven bright stars shaped like a soup ladle. Then imagine a line joining the last two stars and follow it out to find the Pole Star.

Pole Star

Big Dipper

Starry tales

Of the 2,000 stars visible with the naked eye, only a few hundred have proper names. Most of the names come from the myths of the ancient Greeks, who believed the night skies told tales, or from the ancient Arabs, who were avid astronomers.

zoom in on...

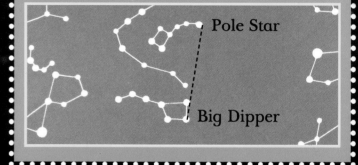

Cygnus the Swan is supposed to be the Greek god Zeus in disguise.

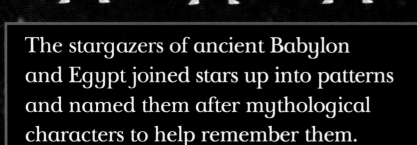

The stargazers of ancient Babylon and Egypt joined stars up into patterns and named them after mythological characters to help remember them. We call these patterns constellations.

Awesome facts
Astronomers use 88 constellations altogether. Most are known by their ancient Greek and Roman names, like Orion the hunter of Greek legend.

Stars in the sky

Look up into the sky on a clear night and you can see lots of twinkling points of light. These twinkling lights are stars like our Sun, only much, much farther away. With a pair of binoculars you can see as many as 5,000 stars! Astronomers guess there are countless trillions out there, too far away to be seen.

Can you spot the Milky Way?

The Milky Way galaxy has 100 billion stars.

Incredible stars

Stars are all huge, fiery balls of gas like our Sun. They shine because they are burning. Because they are so big, pressures deep inside are enough to squeeze atoms so they join together and produce energy called "nuclear fusion"—like a nuclear bomb but billions of times more powerful. The star's center reaches millions of degrees and its surface shines very brightly.

Awesome facts

Inside the biggest stars, temperatures can reach hundreds of millions of degrees, hotter than anything on Earth.

Q: How long have people watched the stars?

A: People have studied the night sky for thousands of years. Some ancient civilizations even thought that the Sun was a god. Early Egyptian astronomers recorded when stars rose and set, and divided the day and night into 12 periods each. They also decorated their temples with constellation gods.

When you look at stars in the sky, their light seems to twinkle and shimmer. Most stars produce an amazingly steady light, but they twinkle because we are seeing them through the thick layers of air above the Earth. When the air moves, the stars seem to shimmer.

Star's light twinkles as it passes through the Earth's atmosphere

The "dog days" are the days in July when Sirius, the

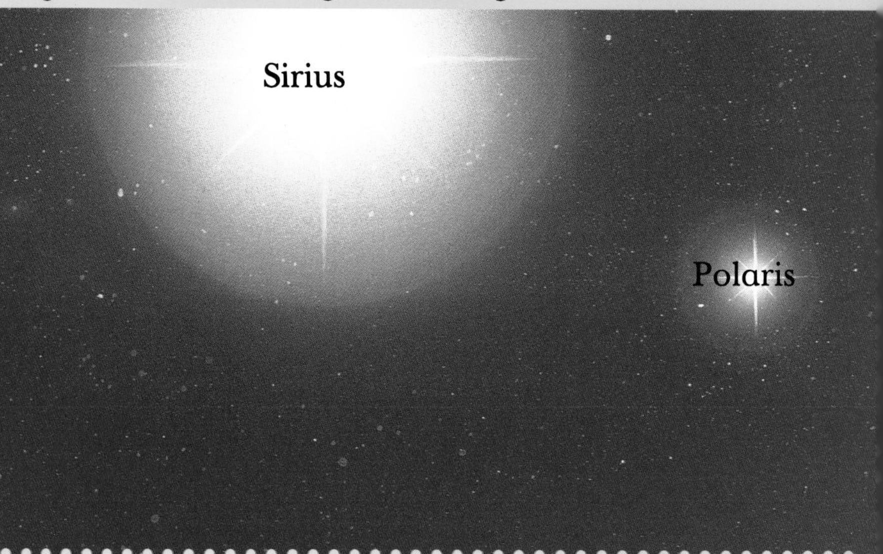

Sirius
Polaris

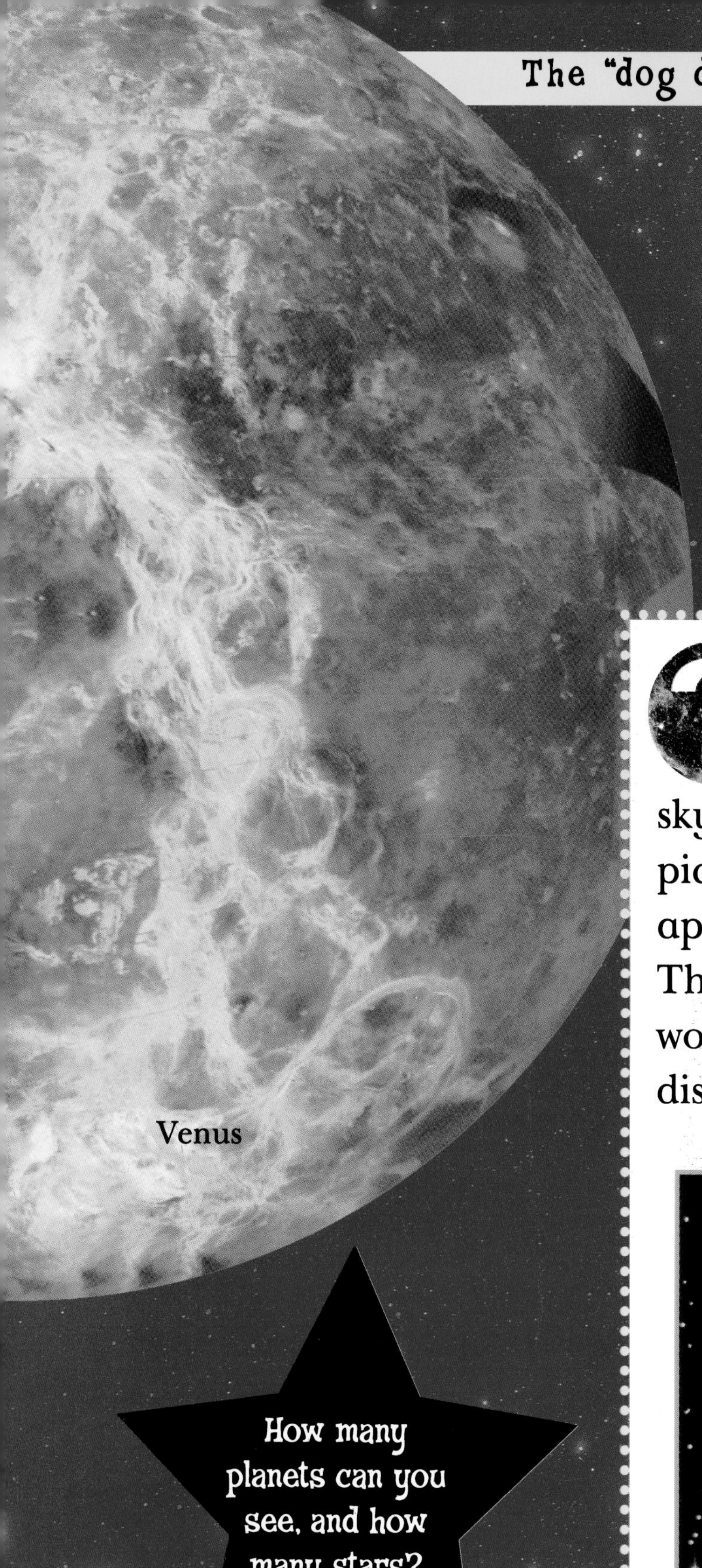

Venus

Q: How bright are Orion's stars?

A: Orion is easy to spot in the night sky since it has several bright stars. The picture below left shows Orion as it appears in the sky (apparent magnitude). The picture below right, shows how Orion would appear if all the stars were the same distance away (absolute magnitude).

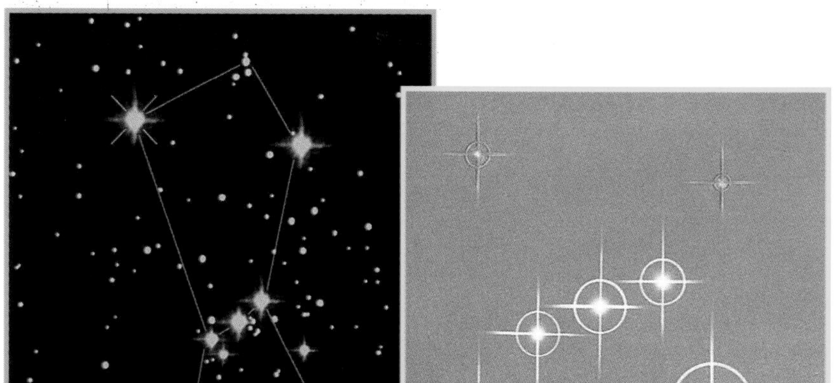

How many planets can you see, and how many stars?

The brightest stars

Some stars seem much brighter than others—sometimes because they are shining brighter, sometimes because they are closer to Earth. A star's "apparent" magnitude is how bright it looks compared to others in the sky. Its "absolute" magnitude tells how bright it really is.

Vega

Spica

Moon

The brighter a star appears, the smaller its apparent magnitude. The brightest thing in the night sky is the Moon, with a magnitude of -12.7. Next comes Venus, which is lit up by the Sun. The brightest star is Sirius. The star Deneb is actually much brighter, but because it is much farther away, it looks dimmer than Sirius.

Moon	-12.7	Vega	0.0
Venus	-4	Polaris	2
Sirius	-1.5	Spica	1.0

21

Awesome factS
Our Sun is an average-sized star—it will burn for about 10 billion years altogether.

Red star

The color of stars

If you look closely at stars, you can see that their colors vary. For example, Rigel is blue, Sirius is white, and Aldebaran is orange. Astronomers have found that the heat, color, and brightness of most stars depend upon each other. Hot stars are usually blue or white, and bright. Medium stars are usually yellow and of medium heat and brightness. Cooler stars are usually orange or red, and dimmer.

Blue star

Yellow star

Q: Can we guess how long a star will live from its color?

A: Yes. Blue stars tend to be brighter, but don't live long. Yellow and white stars will burn for about 10 billion years, while red stars are the coolest and will tend to burn longest.

How far to the stars?

Space is much bigger than you can ever possibly imagine, and the stars are huge distances away. The nearest galaxy to ours, the Andromeda galaxy, is so far away that light takes two million years to reach us from there. This means that when astronomers look at it, they are seeing it as it was over two million years ago!

Moon

Sun

1 second

8 minutes

Earth

Q: What is a quasar?

A: Quasar is short for quasi-stellar object. Quasars are incredibly bright objects that astronomers believe to be at the center of very distant galaxies. They are probably the most distant objects astronomers have ever observed.

24

Light year

Because distances in space are so huge, astronomers measure them in light years rather than miles or kilometers. Light is the fastest thing in the Universe, traveling 186,000 miles (300,000 km) in just one second. A light year is the distance light travels in one year, which is nearly 6 trillion miles (9.5 trillion km).

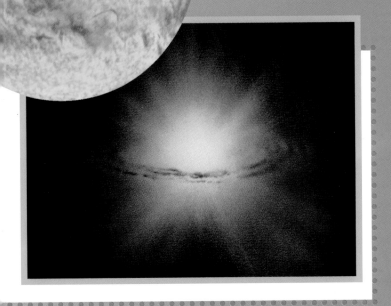

Pluto	Alpha Centauri	Andromeda galaxy
5.5 hours	4.2 light years	2.6 million light years

The illustration shows how long light takes to reach Earth from parts of the Universe. For light, the Moon is just 1.5 seconds away and the Sun is 8 minutes away, but the planet Pluto is 5.5 hours away. The nearest star system, Alpha Centauri, is four years away, and the next galaxy to ours, the Andromeda galaxy, is two million years away!

25

Can you spot the supernovae?

3. Giant star swells to become a supergiant.

4. Medium-sized star collapses to become white dwarf.

2. Giant star starts to swell.

3. Medium-sized star explodes leaving disk of gas and dust.

1. Very bright giant star

2. Medium-sized star swells.

1. Medium-sized star

1. Bright large star

2. Large star starts to swell.

Nebula, the birthplace of stars

4. Giant star explodes in supernova.

5. Giant star collapses and creates black hole.

The life of a star

All stars are born in big clouds of dust and gas called nebulae. Stars burn until their fuel is used up. Giant stars swell to an enormous size, explode in a supernova, and collapse to form a black hole. A large star will do the same, but may create a tiny, dense "neutron star" instead of a black hole. Medium-sized stars will swell and explode to leave a white dwarf. Small stars glow dimly for a long time and then cool and fade to a black dwarf.

5. Collapsed large star ends up as a pulsar or neutron star.

4. Large star explodes in supernova.

3. Large star swells to supergiant.

in on...

Supernova!

In 1054 a huge supernova was seen in many parts of the world. A star scratched into stone by Native Americans has been found in present-day New Mexico and is thought to be a record of this supernova event.

Awesome facts

In 1987, the star SN1987A exploded in a supernova. It burned so brightly that it was visible to the naked eye—even though it is in another galaxy.

In their last moments, big stars swell until they are supergiants. Pressure in the heart of a supergiant is so huge that gravity squeezes the star and it collapses in an instant to something little bigger than the Earth. At once, it explodes, sending a bright ring of debris and an immensely powerful shockwave rippling out.

Exploding superstars

When a giant star runs out of fuel, it swells up, then collapses in an instant, and blows itself to bits in a gigantic "supernova." Supernovae are rare and brief, but when they occur, they are the biggest firework displays in the Universe. They can burn brighter in a few seconds than our Sun does in 200 million years.

Double stars

Some stars exist in pairs that orbit each other. This means that sometimes, seen from Earth, one star may pass in front of the other and their brightness will seem to change, especially when a large dim star passes in front of a small bright one.

Sometimes pairs of stars are so close together that they appear to the naked eye to be a single star. Alpha Centauri is actually a pair of yellow stars that orbit each other, while Albireo (above) in Cygnus is made up of a yellow and a blue star.

When stars orbit each other, one can sometimes eclipse the other. Algol is known as the "winking demon" because as its stars eclipse, it dims and seems to wink.

How many pairs of stars can you spot?

Try this with a friend. When it is dark ask your friend to shine a flashlight on a wall. Walk in a circle around your friend, like a dim star orbiting a bright star. See how you break the beam of light on the wall as you pass in front of it.

Changing stars

While some stars shine steadily, others seem to change in brightness. This can be because two double stars are orbiting each other. However, the actual brightness of a single star can change as well. Giants and supergiants regularly grow larger and smaller and change in color and brightness as they get hotter and colder.

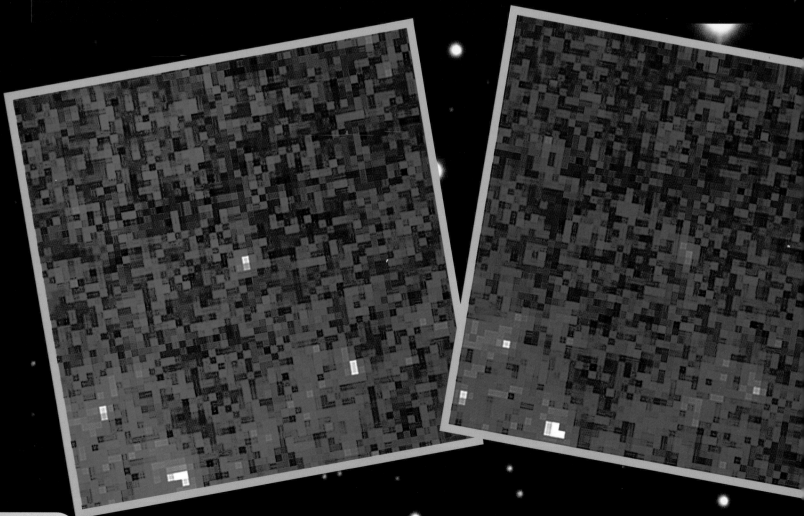

Q: What happens when a star gets old?

A: Toward the end of its life, a star can become unstable. Some old stars will vary in brightness as their fuel supply runs out. They will pulse irregularly for a while before exploding in a giant supernova explosion.

Some stars seem to pulse as their brightness varies. This happens as they expand and contract in size. As a star expands, it becomes colder and dimmer, and as it shrinks it becomes hotter and brighter. Some stars shrink and swell continuously.

Awesome facts

In 1975, before the nova Cygni erupted, it was too faint to be seen. It exploded and increased in brightness 20 million times.

Pulsing pulsars

A small, spinning neutron star sometimes lets off flashes of energy as it spins. The energy can be in the form of radio waves or light waves. If Earth lies in the light beam, we see a flashing light that pulses like the light from a lighthouse. This is why these types of stars are called pulsars.

Pulsar gives off beams of energy.

Awesome facts

The Crab Nebula has a pulsar at the center that flashes 30 times a second.

Crab Nebula

Pulsars

When a giant star explodes in a supernova, it sometimes forms a tiny, spinning neutron star. This neutron star is thought to be the tiny core of the star that has been squashed by the explosion. The neutron star spins very rapidly and sometimes gives out a flash of energy. A flashing neutron star is called a pulsar.

Awesome factS

The Crab Nebula is the remains of the supernova that exploded in 1054, and is still giving off 100,000 times as much energy as the Sun.

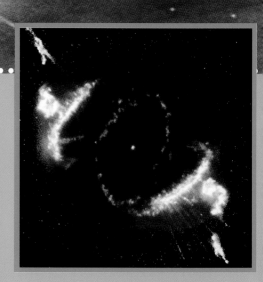

Planetary nebula left behind after a supernova explosion

Q: How many types of nebula are there?

A: Unlike stars, nebulae don't produce light themselves. But reflection nebulae can be seen because the dust in them reflects the light of nearby stars. Glowing nebulae glow red as hydrogen in them is heated by radiation from nearby stars. Planetary nebulae (which have nothing to do with planets) are the flimsy rings of cloud and dust let off when a star dies.

Can you spot the crab's claws?

Giant clouds

On a clear night, you can see a few fuzzy patches of light. Some of these are distant galaxies, but some are gigantic clouds in space called nebulae. Nebulae are clouds of dust and gas. In some nebulae, gravity squeezes the dust and gas tightly together, and stars are formed.

Reflection nebula reflects light from nearby stars.

Glowing nebula gives out light because gas in it is heated.

Mars appears to wander more than any other planet. This is because it orbits the Sun more slowly than the Earth and its orbit is outside the Earth's. As a result, as the Earth catches up and overtakes it, Mars appears to double back on itself.

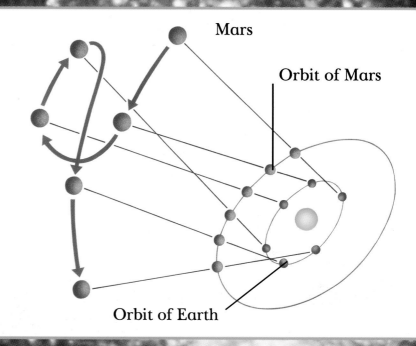

Mars

Orbit of Mars

Orbit of Earth

in on...

How the planets got their name

Long ago, astronomers noticed an odd thing about some of the twinkling lights. They did not stay in the same place like the other stars in the sky, but seemed to wander about. Astronomers called the bodies that moved "planets," which is a Greek word for "wanderers."

Neptune shines because it is lit up by the Sun's light.

Planets or stars?

Planets are large objects like Earth that orbit a star like the Sun. Planets shine because they reflect the light of their star. They do not produce light of their own. Stars produce their own light and heat because of nuclear reactions which take place inside them. The Sun is a star

Closed clusters of stars shine very brightly

Scientists have figured out that the Solar System formed 4.6 billion years ago. At first, it was just a dark, whirling mass of gas and dust. But as it spun, gravity pulled bits tighter together. The dense center became the Sun, and dust farther out came together to form the planets.

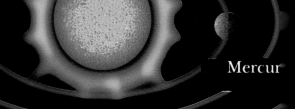

Earth

Sun

Ve

Mercur

Chapter 2

Planets and their moons

The Earth doesn't just hang in space. It zooms at almost 67,000 mph (107,000 km/h) around the Sun. Earth isn't alone. Another eight huge balls, called planets, circle the Sun, too—all held in place by the pull of the Sun's gravity. The Sun, its planets and their moons, and comets and asteroids are together called the Solar System.

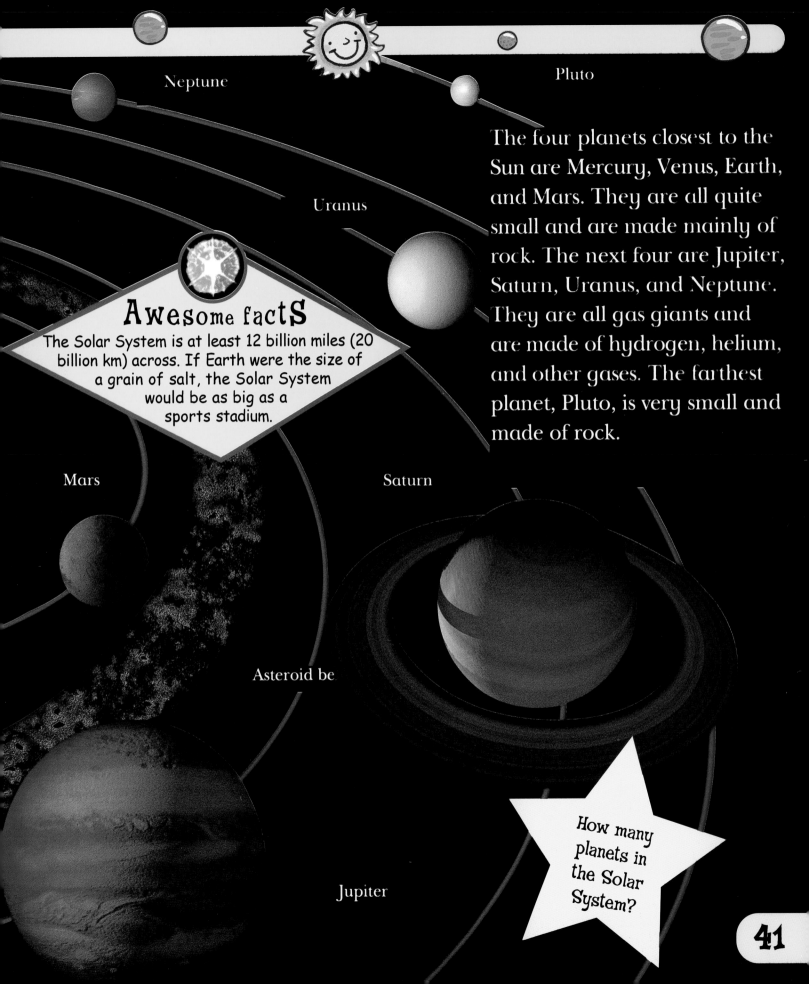

Neptune

Pluto

Uranus

The four planets closest to the Sun are Mercury, Venus, Earth, and Mars. They are all quite small and are made mainly of rock. The next four are Jupiter, Saturn, Uranus, and Neptune. They are all gas giants and are made of hydrogen, helium, and other gases. The farthest planet, Pluto, is very small and made of rock.

Awesome facts

The Solar System is at least 12 billion miles (20 billion km) across. If Earth were the size of a grain of salt, the Solar System would be as big as a sports stadium.

Mars

Saturn

Asteroid belt

How many planets in the Solar System?

Jupiter

zoom in on...

Mercury's surface

Mercury is small, so its gravity is very weak and can't hold onto an atmosphere. So there is nothing to protect the planet from the Sun's rays or to stop meteoroids from bashing into it. As a result, it is deeply dented with craters like the Moon. A journey across the surface would show you nothing more than vast, empty basins, cliffs hundreds of miles long, and yellow dust everywhere.

Earth

Mercury

Mercury is smaller than some of Jupiter's moons. It is 20 times lighter than Earth and barely a third of the diameter.

Q: If Mercury takes 59 days to turn around, how come the Sun stays up for 176 days?

A: Mercury rotates slowly, but whizzes around the Sun in just 88 days (compared to 365 days for Earth). This means that as it turns slowly away from the Sun, it whizzes around the other side, so that the sunny side is still facing the Sun.

Mercury

Mercury is the nearest planet to the Sun, often less than 36 million miles (58 million km) away. Mercury has little atmosphere, so the side facing the Sun can be more than 800°F (430°C), while the dark side is an icy cold -290°F (-180°C).

Earth turns once around on its axis in 23 hours 56 minutes. Mercury takes nearly 59 Earth days to turn once around its axis.

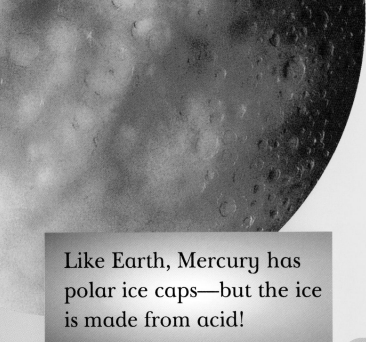

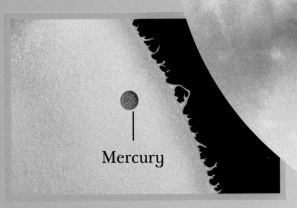

Mercury

Every so often, Mercury passes across the face of the Sun when seen from the Earth.

Like Earth, Mercury has polar ice caps—but the ice is made from acid!

Venus

Venus is almost exactly the same size as Earth. It measures about 7,500 miles (12,000 km) across and weighs just a little less than Earth. It is sometimes called the Evening Star or the Morning Star. This is because it is quite close to the Sun, so it can be seen in the night sky just after sunset or just before sunrise.

zoom in on...

Atmosphere

Venus is a beautiful planet covered in swirls of pinkish white cloud. But the pink clouds are actually made partly of sulfuric acid. They are so thick that they press down on the planet's surface hard enough to crush a car!

Venus

Moon

When our Moon is a new crescent moon, it is between the Earth and the Sun. Venus lies between the Earth and the Sun, too. So sometimes you will see Venus near the new Moon as it rises.

44

The surface of Venus can't be seen since it is hidden behind swirls of pinkish white cloud. It has probably always been too hot for water ever to have existed there. All that is left are hot, bone-dry, rolling plains dotted with volcanoes and vast plateaus.

Computer reconstruction of Venus's surface

Awesome factS

Carbon dioxide in Venus's atmosphere traps heat on the surface, boosting the temperature as high as 878°F (470°C), the hottest in the Solar System.

Planet Earth

Earth is the third planet out from the Sun, about 93 million miles (150 million km) away. It is not so close to the Sun that it is scorching hot, nor so far away that it is icy cold. It has water on its surface, and can sustain life.

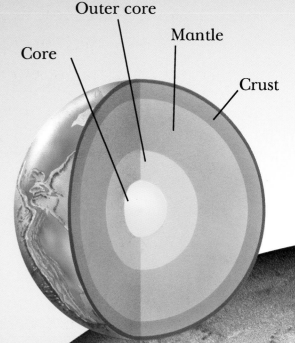

Core   Outer core   Mantle   Crust

Q: Why can we live on our planet?

A: Earth is a special place. It is the only planet that we know has water on its surface, and water makes life possible. It also has a blanket of gases, called the atmosphere, which we breathe.

The Earth is made mainly of rock and is the densest planet in the Solar System. But it is not just a solid ball. It has a shell, or crust, of hard rock. Beneath that is a layer about 1,850 miles (3,000 km) deep of warm, partly melted rock, called the mantle. The center is a core made entirely of hot metal, mostly iron.

**zoom in on...**

Earth is not round!

Earth is not quite round. It bulges at the middle, around the equator. Going through Earth from pole to pole is 27 miles (43 km) shorter than going between opposite points on the equator.

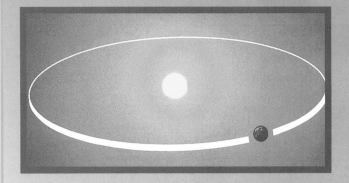

Earth whizzes once around the Sun every year. It is slightly tilted over. So, as it travels around the Sun, the zone on Earth tilted toward the Sun gradually shifts. This is what creates seasons—the part of the world tilted toward the Sun has summer, the part which is tilted away has winter. The equator has no seasons.

70% of Earth is ocean. Can you spot the land?

Our Moon

The Moon is Earth's closest companion. It is about 240,000 miles (384,400 km) away. The Moon circles around Earth about once a month—which is how we got the word "month" (or "moonth").

The Moon seems to change shape over a month. We only see the side of the Moon that is lit by the Sun. As the Moon circles Earth, we see it from different angles—and so see more or less of its sunlit side.

At the new moon (1), we see a thin crescent-shaped sliver. This grows over the next two weeks to a full moon (3), when we see all the sunlit side. It then shrinks back over the rest of the month to a crescent-shape—the old moon (5).

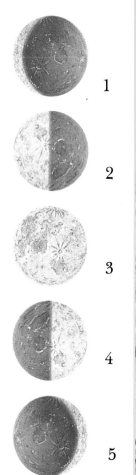

1

2

3

4

5

The Moon is a barren, lifeless place covered with dust and craters caused by huge meteorites crashing into it billions of years ago.

Q: How was the Moon made?

A: Amazingly, the Moon was probably made by a space collision. About 4.5 billion years ago, soon after the Earth formed, a planet at least as big as Mars collided with Earth. The crash completely melted the other planet, and splashes flew off into space. Gradually, gravity pulled these splashes together into a ball, which cooled to form the Moon.

A large object hits the Earth. The object melts and splashes of debris fly into space.

Debris spins in orbit and joins together to form the Moon.

Awesome facts

There are huge dark patches on the Moon called seas which have never had a drop of water. They are plains formed long ago by hot, molten rock from the Moon's inside.

Craters on
Mars's surface

zoom in on...

Water on Mars?

In the 1880s, astronomers
thought dark lines they saw
on Mars's surface were actually canals built
by Martians. They proved to be optical
illusions, but valleys show water once
flowed over the surface in abundance.

Valley on
Mars's surface

Mars

Mars is the only planet to have an atmosphere or daytime temperatures anything like ours. But Mars is a desert planet, with no oceans or any sign of life—just red rocks and dust and a pink sky.

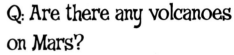
Ice-covered pole

Q: Are there any volcanoes on Mars?

A: Like Earth and Venus, Mars has volcanoes. In fact, Olympus Mons (below) on Mars is the biggest volcano in the Solar System—three times higher than Mount Everest!

More spacecraft have landed on Mars than on any planet. In 1997, the Mars Pathfinder landed and sent out a robot truck to scan the area and beam back TV pictures. In the near future, missions to Mars hope to probe beneath the surface to search for signs of microscopic life.

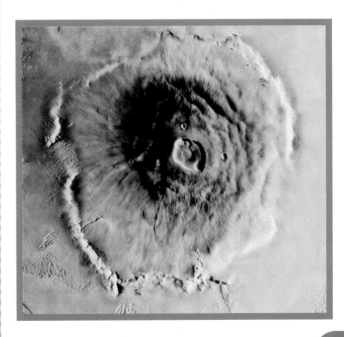

Jupiter's gravity is so powerful that it squeezes hydrogen and helium gases until they become liquid or solid. Under the thin atmosphere is an ocean of liquid hydrogen and a small rocky core.

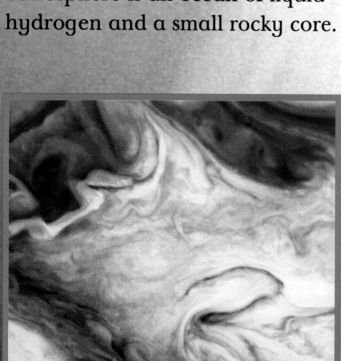

Jupiter weighs 318 times as much as Earth. Its colorful clouds are whipped into long belts by violent winds up to 300 miles per hour (500 km/h).

Awesome factS

Jupiter revolves once in 10 Earth hours, compared to 24 hours for Earth. Jupiter's equator is revolving at 30,000 miles per hour (47,000 km/h)!

Jupiter

Jupiter is gigantic. It is by far the biggest planet in the Solar System—over 88,000 miles (140,000 km) across—and it takes 12 years to go around the Sun. It is an enormous ball of gas, more like the Sun than like the Earth, and is made mainly of hydrogen and helium. You can see it clearly for part of the year—it is brighter than any of the stars.

Find the Great Red Spot.

Q: What is the red spot?

A: The Great Red Spot, or GRS, is a dark red swirl of clouds in Jupiter's atmosphere that was first noticed more than 300 years ago. It seems to be a gigantic hurricane, with very strong winds.

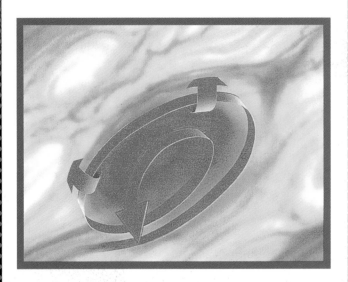

If you were on Ganymede, you would see Jupiter in the sky.

Jupiter's moons

Jupiter has at least 16 moons. The four largest (Io, Europa, Ganymede, and Callisto) were discovered by the scientist Galileo in 1610. Ganymede and Callisto are larger than our own Moon, and the other two are not much smaller.

Ganymede

Awesome factS
Jupiter has 16 known moons, but there may be others too small to have been seen yet. You can see the four biggest moons with an ordinary pair of binoculars!

Until Galileo saw through his telescope that Jupiter's moons circled around it, people thought that everything in the Universe circled around our Earth.

Europa

Callisto

Io

Europa's oceans

Europa has a very bright, smooth surface of ice, possibly with liquid water beneath. Scientists think that there might be life forms in this water. In places, the surface of Europa is cracked like an eggshell.

Io has been called the most volcanic body in the Solar System. When the Voyager 2 space probe passed it in 1979, it discovered that plumes of material were being shot out from Io's surface up to a height of nearly 200 miles (300 km). It was the first evidence of active volcanoes anywhere other than Earth.

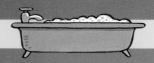

Changing rings

1995

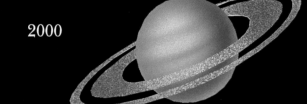

2000

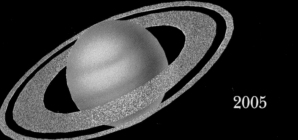

2005

2009

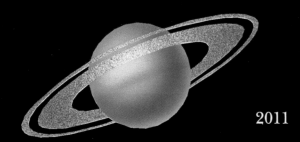

2011

Awesome factS

When Galileo first discovered Saturn's rings in 1610, he thought the planet had "ears" or "handles" because his telescope wasn't sharp enough.

We see Saturn at different angles at different times, so we can see Saturn's rings better at some times than others. In 1995, the rings were edge on and hard to see. In 2005, they will be at a greater angle, giving us a clear view.

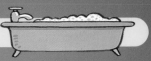

Saturn

Saturn is the second largest planet, a gas giant over 74,000 miles (120,000 km) across. Saturn is known as the Ringed Planet because around it circle amazing rings stretching out 43,000 miles (70,000 km). Saturn's core is made of rock twice as hot as the Sun's surface.

 Q: What are Saturn's rings made of?

A: Saturn's rings are bands of countless billions of tiny blocks of ice and dust, circling the planet endlessly. Each ring is thousands of miles wide.

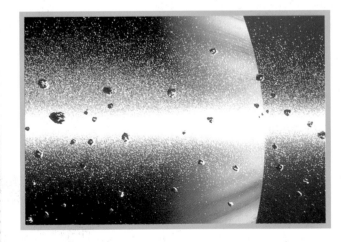

Iapetus

zoom in on...

Phoebe's orbit

Most of Saturn's moons circle quite close. They all orbit outside Saturn's rings. Phoebe orbits the farthest out, much farther than the other moons, taking 550 days to go around once. It also orbits backward, in an opposite direction to the other moons.

Phoebe

Dione

Saturn

Awesome facts

One of Saturn's moons, Iapetus has one side which is dark black like tar, while the other side is white as snow.

Titan

Saturn's moons

More moons have been discovered around Saturn than around any other planet, at least 22, and there are probably more smaller ones still to be discovered. Titan is the largest of all Saturn's moons, and is the second largest moon in the Solar System after Jupiter's moon Ganymede.

How many moons can you see?

Saturn's moon Mimas shows clearly a huge crater called the Herschel crater. The impact that made the crater would have been so strong that it almost broke Mimas apart.

Mimas

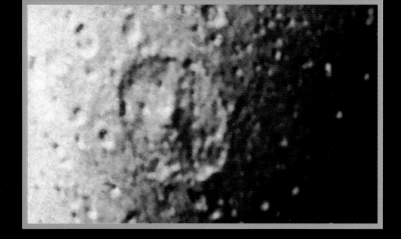

Tethys

Uranus

Uranus is so far from the Sun that temperatures on its surface drop to -346°F (-210°C). In this amazing cold, the methane (natural gas) that covers the planet turns to liquid oceans thousands of miles deep. It is the methane gas that gives Uranus its beautiful blue color.

Uranus tilts so far that it's on its side. It spins around once every 17 hours, but this has no effect on the length of a day. Instead, the day depends on where Uranus is in its orbit. When the south pole is pointing directly at the Sun, the Sun doesn't go down there for 20 years!

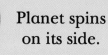

Planet spins on its side.

Sun

Awesome facts

Because Uranus rolls around the Sun on its side, the Sun does some odd things. In spring, the Sun rises and sets every nine hours—backward.

Uranus's icy atmosphere is made of hydrogen and helium. Winds whistle through it at over 1,250 mph (2,000 km/h), ten times faster than the fastest hurricane on Earth. If you fell into its icy oceans for even a fraction of a second, you'd freeze so hard you could be shattered like glass.

Uranus's moon, Oberon

 zoom in on...

Long year

Uranus is almost 2 billion miles (3 billion km) from the Sun. This far out, the distance Uranus has to travel around the Sun is vast—and takes more than 84 Earth years. So on Uranus, you'd be collecting your pension on your first birthday.

Neptune

Neptune is the fourth-largest planet in the Solar System. It's so far from the Sun—about 2.8 billion miles (4.5 billion km)—that it takes 164.79 years to go around the Sun. Indeed, it hasn't even gone around once since it was first discovered back in 1846.

Cloud features on Neptune's surface

zoom in on...

Scooter

Neptune has raging storms and clouds on its surface that come and go over the years, probably driven by Neptune's internal heat. It also has a small white cloud of methane ice crystals that zips around the planet once every 16 hours and so is now known as the Scooter.

Great Dark Spot can sometimes be seen on Neptune's surface.

Neptune is an icy blue planet with an atmosphere like Uranus, and covered in oceans of liquid methane. On Neptune, surface temperatures plunge to -330°F (-201°C)—but its moon Triton is even colder, with temperatures a chilling -393°F (-236°C). Triton's surface is covered in volcanoes that erupt—ice!

Triton

Surface of Triton

Can you spot the clouds on Neptune's surface?

Pluto

Pluto is the most remote planet in the Solar System—a tiny, lonely world smaller than our Moon. It is so far from the Sun that the Sun looks little bigger than a star in the sky. Sunlight only takes eight minutes to reach Earth, but takes up to six hours to reach Pluto.

Pluto has a moon almost half its size, called Charon. Pluto and Charon circle around each other, locked together in space like a weightlifter's dumbbells. So Charon always stays in the same place in Pluto's sky, looking eight times as big as our Moon.

Q: How big is Pluto compared to Earth?

A: Pluto is only 1,432 miles (2,274 km) across, barely a fifth of the size of Earth. Because it is so small and hard to spot, Pluto was discovered only in 1930.

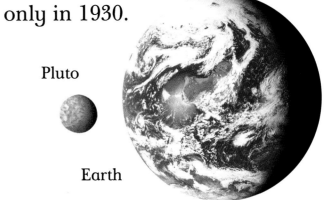

Pluto

Earth

zoom in on...

Charlene!

The man who found Charon in 1978 was going to call it after his wife, Charlene. But he chose Charon after the ferryman who took lost souls to the Greek underworld, land of Pluto.

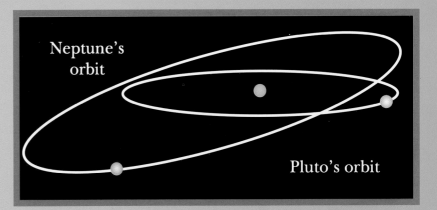

Neptune's orbit

Pluto's orbit

Pluto has an odd oval orbit. Most of the time, it is billions of miles out beyond Neptune. But for several years every three centuries, it actually moves in closer to the Sun than Neptune.

Asteroids

In addition to the nine planets in the Solar System, there is a lot of debris. Hundreds of thousands of tiny pieces of rock, metal, and ice whizz around the Sun. Some of these pieces are asteroids, which are mainly found in the asteroid belt between Mars and Jupiter. Some, called Near Earth Objects (NEOs), come close to Earth.

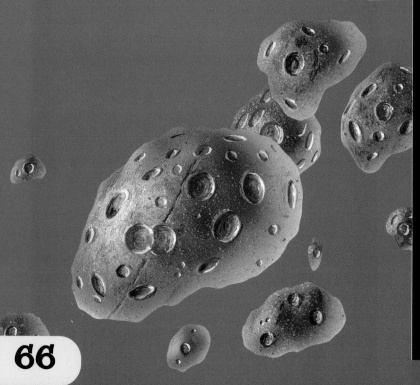

When asteroids collide, pieces of rock or iron break off, forming many smaller asteroids. Some asteroids are tiny, but the biggest asteroid, Ceres, is 580 miles (933 km) across —that's almost a third of the size of our Moon. The asteroid Ida has its own moon called Dactyl, which is just 1 mile (1.6 km) wide.

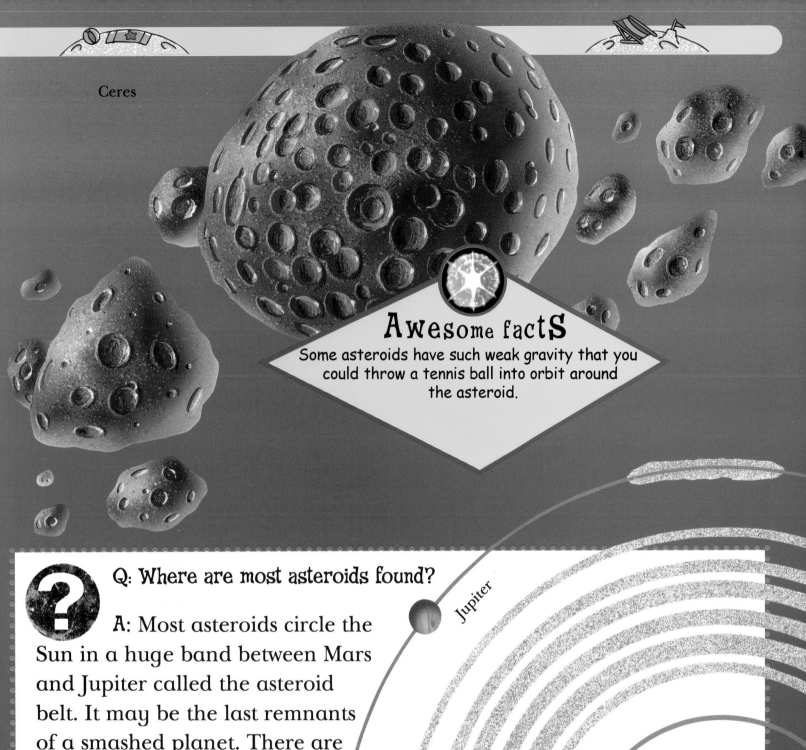

Ceres

Awesome facts

Some asteroids have such weak gravity that you could throw a tennis ball into orbit around the asteroid.

Q: Where are most asteroids found?

A: Most asteroids circle the Sun in a huge band between Mars and Jupiter called the asteroid belt. It may be the last remnants of a smashed planet. There are 26 asteroids that are over 125 miles (200 km) across, over a million that are at least a mile (1 km) across, and billions of smaller bits!

Jupiter

Sun

Mars

Comets

Comets are like huge dirty snowballs that orbit in the outer reaches of the Solar System. A comet's core is just a few miles across, but when it swings in close to the Sun and partly melts, it throws out a vast tail of dust and gas.

 Q: How long have we known about comets?

A: Halley's Comet appears in the Bayeux Tapestry, which depicts the Battle of Hastings in 1066, but records show that the comet was spotted as long ago as 240 BC.

In July 1994, people on Earth watched as fragments of the comet Shoemaker-Levy 9 collided with Jupiter. The comet's impact could be clearly seen on the planet's surface.

Q: What are comets made of?

A: The center of a comet is a hard core made of ice, frozen gases, and pieces of rock and dust. Around the core are layers of ice and rock. It is surrounded by an outer crust.

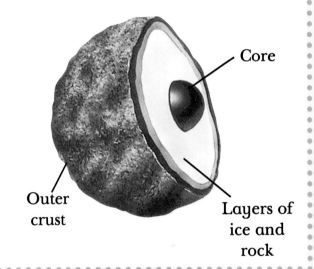

Core

Outer crust

Layers of ice and rock

Halley's Comet appears in our sky every 76 years or so. In 1986, the space probe Giotto was sent up to visit Halley's Comet when it flew past the Earth. It flew through the tail of the comet, taking photographs as it went.

A meteorite is space debris that has fallen to Earth, sometimes leaving a large hole or crater. Most meteorites are quite small and are made of stone or iron. Museums keep collections of meteorites that you can go and see.

Meteoroids and shooting stars

A meteoroid is dirt or debris from an asteroid or comet. It can be seen as a meteor, or shooting star, as it burns in the Earth's atmosphere. Most burn away before they fall to Earth. When meteors fall to Earth, they are called meteorites, and are usually no bigger than a lump of coal.

Awesome factS

It is thought that the impact of a huge meteorite 65 million years ago may have changed conditions on Earth so much that it killed off the dinosaurs.

If you look into the night sky at any time of the year, you may see some shooting stars. However, the best time to see good showers of them in the northern hemisphere is in the first part of August.

Q: Where can we see a big meteorite crater?

A: The Meteor Crater in Arizona is a vast bowl that formed when a meteorite crashed there 50,000 years ago. The impact created a hole nearly 4,000 feet (1,200 m) across and 650 feet (200 m) deep.

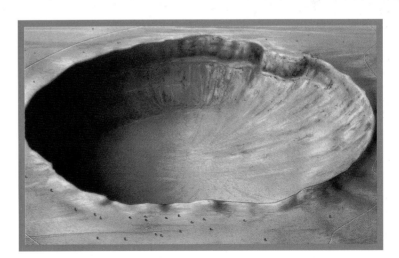

Chapter 3

Space exploration

Every year scientists probe farther and farther into space. Using telescopes, robot probes, rockets, and satellites, they have explored moons, planets, stars, galaxies, and beyond.

Astronomers use powerful telescopes to study the night sky. As telescopes become more and more powerful, astronomers can see millions of previously unseen stars and galaxies. Telescopes in space have even captured images of galaxies millions of light years away.

Scientists send robot probes into space to gather information about the Universe. Some have flown past the planets and beamed back spectacular images of their surfaces and moons, while other probes have actually landed on some planets, and transmitted back live TV pictures.

The Space Shuttle hitches a ride into space on the back of a rocket.

Galileo visited Jupiter in 1995.

Powerful rockets are sent into space on different types of mission. Some carry satellites to be released into orbit, and others carry astronauts on space journeys.

Observatories

Astronomers study the stars from buildings called observatories. These are often built on mountaintops away from low clouds and city lights to give a clear view of the night sky.

Awesome facts

The world's largest observatory is 13,800 feet (4,200 m) high, near the top of Mauna Kea in Hawaii.

Observatory

An observatory is a building that houses a telescope. Most have a domed roof that rotates with the telescope during the night so that it can keep aiming at the same stars as the Earth rotates.

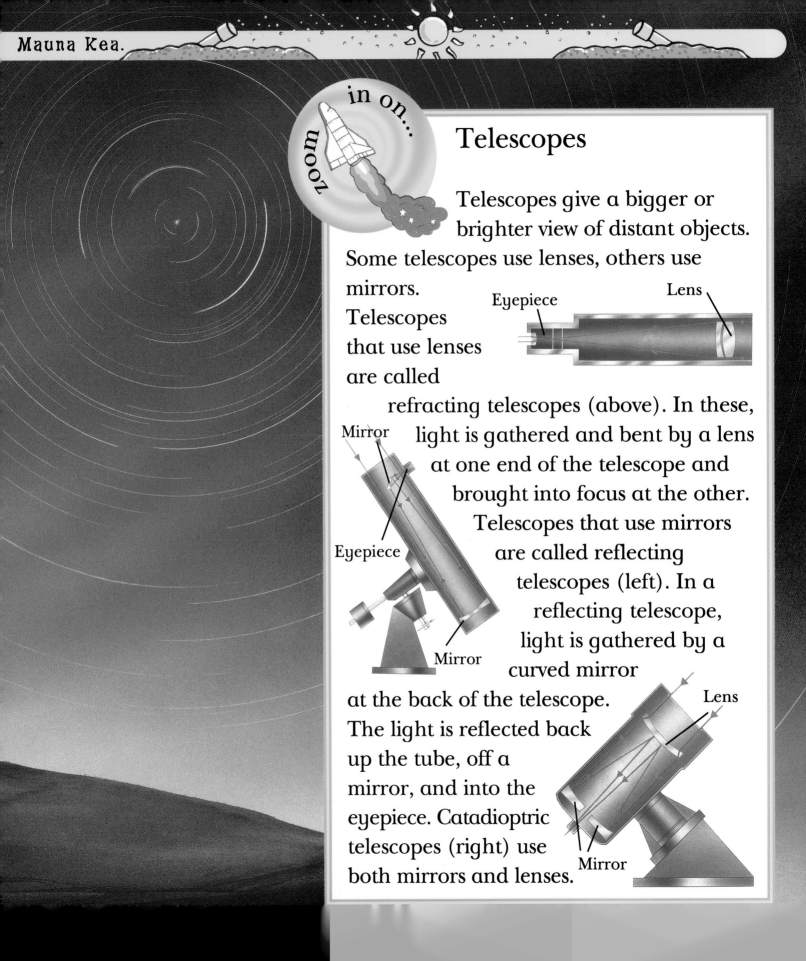

zoom in on...

Telescopes

Telescopes give a bigger or brighter view of distant objects. Some telescopes use lenses, others use mirrors. Telescopes that use lenses are called refracting telescopes (above). In these, light is gathered and bent by a lens at one end of the telescope and brought into focus at the other. Telescopes that use mirrors are called reflecting telescopes (left). In a reflecting telescope, light is gathered by a curved mirror at the back of the telescope. The light is reflected back up the tube, off a mirror, and into the eyepiece. Catadioptric telescopes (right) use both mirrors and lenses.

Eyepiece

Lens

Mirror

Eyepiece

Mirror

Lens

Mirror

Space telescopes

A position in orbit offers a much better view of space because it is above the clouds and haze of Earth's atmosphere. Space telescopes have already shown many things we could never see from Earth, even through the most powerful telescopes.

 Q: How did Hubble get into space?

A: The Hubble Space Telescope was carried into space by the Space Shuttle. It was unloaded in space by the shuttle astronauts and sent into orbit. It is still beaming back amazing pictures to us from space.

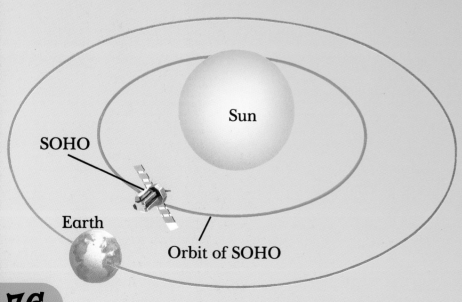

Sun

SOHO

Earth

Orbit of SOHO

SOHO (Solar and Heliospheric Observatory) was designed to study the Sun and was launched into orbit between the Earth and the Sun so that its view of the Sun was uninterrupted. Among other things, SOHO has studied the Sun's surface, sunspots, and the Sun's insides.

The most famous of the space telescopes now orbiting the Earth is the Hubble Space Telescope (HST), launched in 1990. The HST has a reflecting telescope which can see five times more detail than any ground-based telescope.

The world's biggest single radio telescope dish is the Arecibo telescope in Puerto Rico. It is a vast, smooth concrete dish 1,000 feet (305 m) across, set into a natural hollow in the top of a mountain. Such a huge dish can pick up even very faint radio signals from space.

How many dishes can you see?

Radio telescopes

We can see the visible light that stars give off, but they also give off other rays, such as radio waves and X-rays, which our eyes cannot detect. Radio telescopes are able to pick up radio rays from a long distance.

Radio telescopes look like huge TV satellite dishes. They pick up radio signals from space. Because radio waves are much longer than light waves, radio telescope dishes have to be much much bigger than ordinary telescopes. Many are more than 300 feet (100 m) across. Several smaller radio telescopes can be linked together so that they work as a single large telescope.

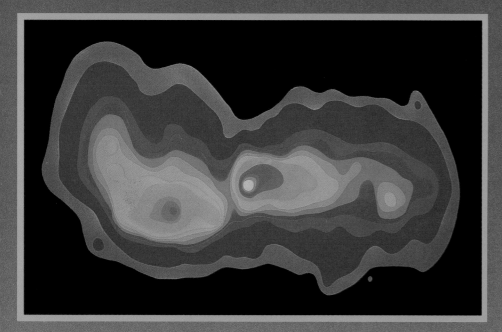

Rockets

Escaping the pull of the Earth's gravity demands enormous power. Special engines called rockets are used to get a spacecraft to a speed great enough to blast clear of Earth.

Command module

Service module

Apollo lunar module

Satellite released into orbit

Rockets need an enormous amount of fuel to get into orbit. They are basically giant fuel tanks. The Saturn 5, which carried the Apollo spacecraft and astronauts to the Moon, was over 360 feet (110 m) tall. The command, service, and lunar modules sat on top of three stages. When one stage was exhausted, it fell away and the next rocket stage took over.

USA

Nose cone falls away.

Spacecraft are usually boosted into space by powerful "launch vehicles" that provide the power for the takeoff thrust. These are rockets in three or four parts or stages. Each stage is designed to fall away once the craft has reached a certain height or speed.

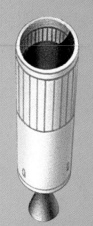

Third stage

Second stage

zoom in on...

Rocket engines

Most big rockets are powered by liquid fuels. In order to burn, the fuel needs oxygen, so rockets also carry a supply of liquid oxygen as well as the fuel they need. The fuel and oxygen mix in a combustion chamber and burn with explosive force, driving the spacecraft forward.

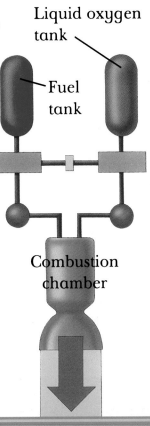

Liquid oxygen tank

Fuel tank

Combustion chamber

First stage boosters fall away.

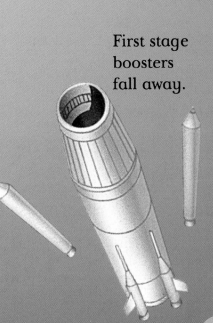

81

Once in space, the craft needs much less fuel and smaller rockets which maneuver and steer in different directions. The spacecraft that continues on the journey after all the launch rockets have fallen away is usually tiny—typically less than a tenth of the size it was on the ground.

Astronauts orbiting the Earth are weightless. They can float around the cabin from one place to another. To sleep, they must fasten themselves to their bed, or they will float away in the night.

Space flights

Once a spacecraft has escaped the Earth's gravity, it can travel huge distances using very little power. It uses small booster rockets, which help it to steer and give it a push in the right direction. With little friction in space, it can "coast" for long distances.

Q: What is escape velocity?

A: Spacecraft can only break free of the Earth's gravity and venture out into space if they can reach a speed of 25,000 miles per hour (40,000 km/h). This is called escape velocity. If a craft reaches a somewhat lower speed, it goes into orbit around Earth, held there by the Earth's strong gravity.

The Shuttle blasts off with five engines. Two booster engines and the main fuel tank fall away in stages. When its mission is finished, it corrects its path and reenters the Earth's atmosphere. It then glides back to Earth, landing like an airplane.

3. Fuel tank falls away.

4. Shuttle deploys satellite.

5. Shuttle maneuvers to correct angle for reentry.

6. Reentry

2. Boosters fall away at 30 miles (45 km) above the ground.

7. Shuttle glides back to Earth so it can be reused.

1. Launch

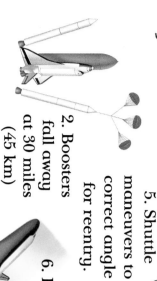

Space shuttle

The Space Shuttle is a unique spacecraft because it can be launched again and again. It can ferry scientists to space laboratories, launch small satellites, or carry crews to repair satellites already in orbit.

zoom in on ...

Shuttle engines

The shuttle craft left once the launch rockets have fallen away is called the orbiter. Once the orbiter is in space, it has only small rockets that steer and maneuver it onto the right course.

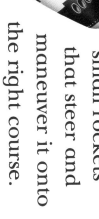

Can you see the rocket boosters?

Many satellites are used for communication, transmitting anything from television pictures to telephone messages. A telephone conversation from New York to Australia, for instance, can be beamed up to a satellite high above the Earth, bounced on to another, and beamed back down to Earth again instantly.

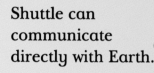

Awesome facts

There have now been over 5,000 satellites in space. Many of them are now useless bits of space junk.

Shuttle can communicate directly with Earth.

When Shuttle is out of sight, signals can be bounced off a relay shuttle.

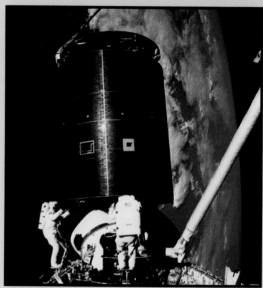

Signals can be received almost instantly thousands of miles away.

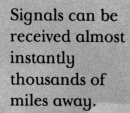

Most satellites only go into orbits less than 200 miles (300 km) high. Some are placed in space by the Space Shuttle. Shuttle astronauts can also carry out repairs on these low-orbiting satellites.

Satellites

An artificial satellite is a spacecraft that orbits a planet. Satellites can send information to astronomers on Earth and can beam TV pictures around the world.

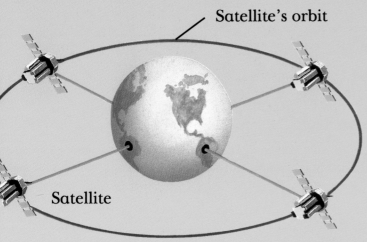

Satellite's orbit

Satellite

When launching a satellite, space scientists set its orbit exactly. If it orbits 22,237 miles (35,786 km) above the Earth, and is traveling at the same speed as the Earth is revolving, it stays over the same point on Earth all the time.

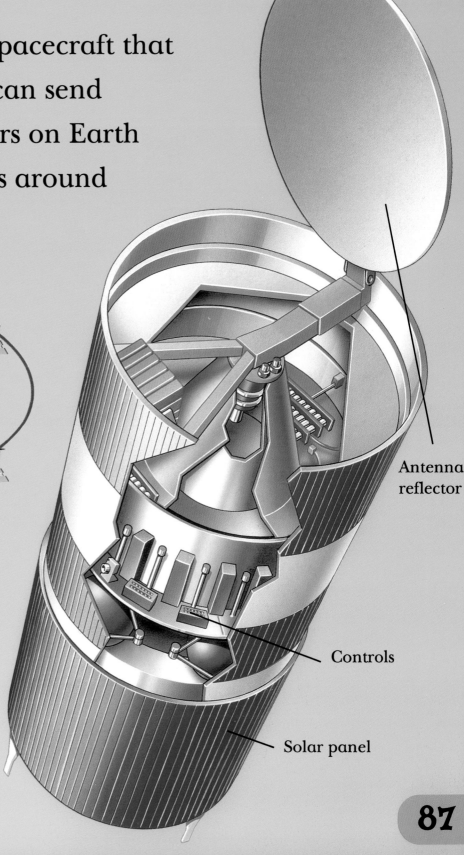

Antenna reflector

Controls

Solar panel

Astronauts

Training for space missions is long and tough. Astronauts must be able to handle many kinds of equipment. They must also be healthy and strong to cope with weightlessness and spacewalks.

zoom in on...

Growing in space

When you sleep, gravity stops pressing your backbones together, so you are a little taller in the morning. The same thing happens to astronauts in space, where gravity doesn't press at all.

Weightlessness makes astronauts feel sick until they get used to it. Before going into space, they train in airplanes that are diving toward the Earth, or underwater to learn how to work in weightlessness.

88

On spacewalks, astronauts wear a special suit that provides Earthlike conditions —air pressure, oxygen to breathe, and warmth. A rocket-powered backpack, or Manned Maneuvering Unit (MMU), can help them move around.

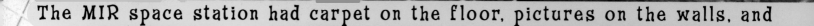
Q: What was Skylab made of?

A: Skylab was made from the third-stage casing of the Saturn V rocket. Launched in 1973, it was in orbit for six years. When it reentered the atmosphere, parts that didn't burn up landed in Australia.

zoom in on...

Living in space

The crew of a space station has to get used to living in weightless conditions. Even simple things must be planned carefully. Food and drink are taken from pouches. Otherwise they would float off their plates and out of their glasses and make a mess in the cabin. Astronauts also need exercise, so spacecraft are fitted with special exercise equipment.

Space stations

The International Space Station (ISS) is a huge space station that is being built in space. It will be as big as two jumbo jets, and when it is finished, it will be used for experiments in space. A crew of up to six people will live on board.

Can you see the solar panels that provide energy?

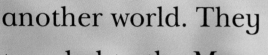

Moon landings

In July 1969, American astronauts set foot on the Moon. It was the first time humans had ever stepped onto another world. They traveled to the Moon in Apollo 11, which was launched on the Saturn V rocket.

Awesome facts

In 1997, the Lunar Prospector discovered ice in the craters at the Moon's poles. This may have come from impacts of comets.

Between 1969 and 1972, the United States landed 12 astronauts on the Moon as part of the Apollo space mission. The astronauts explored different regions, taking samples of rock and recording the amazing scenes that they discovered.

On the last three Apollo missions, the astronauts even had a buggy to carry them and their equipment around. The Apollo Lunar Rover looked like a simple dune buggy and was able to carry two people. It was powered by electric motors. It could travel at about 10 mph (15 km/h).

Mercury has been visited only by Mariner 10, which flew past it three times in 1974 and 1975. It got to within 180 miles (300 km) of the surface, but was able to map less than half of the planet. It found that Mercury's surface is much like the surface of the Moon, covered in rocky craters thought to be from impacts millions of years ago.

zoom in on...

Mars visit

A recent Mars mission was the American Mars Pathfinder expedition, which landed on July 4, 1997. Pathfinder bounced onto Mars's surface, protected by airbags. The probe then released a small robot vehicle called Sojourner, which could be remotely-controlled. It was used to explore the Martian landscape.

Visiting the inner planets

Mercury and Venus are difficult to observe from Earth. Mercury is very close to the Sun, and Venus is covered in thick clouds of gas. The only details of these planets have been supplied by probes. Mars is easier to explore and is the most visited of all the planets.

Can you see the space probe Venera?

Many missions have flown past Venus. A few have succeeded in landing on the planet's surface to send back data about its harsh conditions. In 1990, the U.S. Magellan probe peered through the thick clouds of Venus's atmosphere to map the planet's surface by radar. It found mountains and volcanoes up to 5 miles (8 km) high.

Venera

Visiting the outer planets

Voyages to the outer planets—Jupiter, Saturn, Uranus, Neptune, and Pluto—are much harder. The distances are huge, which means radio communications take several hours, and the probes must pass through hazardous radiation belts near Jupiter.

Voyager 2 visited Saturn and examined its rings and moons, then went on to Uranus, but revealed little detail. It continued on to Neptune, where it revealed storms in the atmosphere.

Voyager

Jupiter was first visited by the American Pioneer 10 probe in 1973. Pioneer 11 first reached Saturn in 1979. The first good images of these planets came from Voyager probes in 1979-81. They took close-ups of Jupiter's moons and surface and showed that Io, one of Jupiter's moons, had active volcanoes on its surface.

Pioneer

The Pioneer and Voyager probes went to the outer planets of the Solar System using the slingshot effect. Each spacecraft flew close to a planet and used the planet's speed around the Sun to propel it farther out into the Solar System.

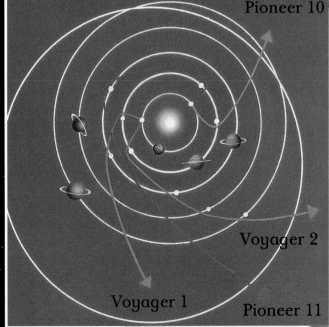

Pioneer 10

Voyager 2

Voyager 1

Pioneer 11

The search for life

Scientists are continually searching the skies for signs of other life forms. Arecibo, the enormous radio telescope in Puerto Rico, receives signals from space, listening for signs that there are other life forms in space.

Q: Will we find another civilization out there?

A: Humans are exploring farther and farther into space with telescopes, probes, and rockets, making new discoveries all the time. Nobody knows whether there are any extraterrestrial civilizations, but we keep looking and listening.

Scientists have discovered a crust of ice on Europa, one of Jupiter's moons. They believe that this crust could cover an ocean, which may contain life forms. For this reason, scientists want to drill under the ice on Europa to see if any life exists there.

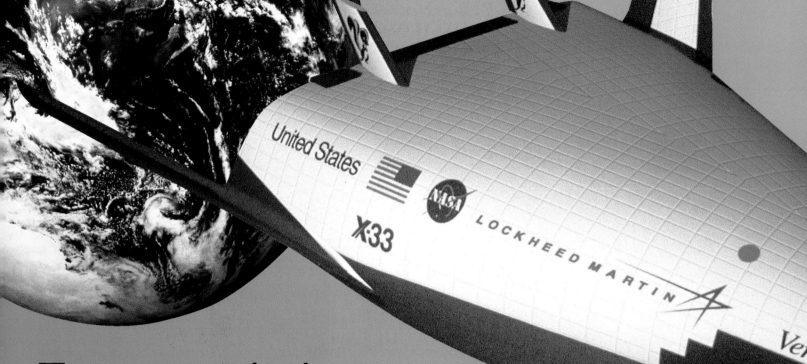

Future missions

The future holds many new and exciting developments in space exploration. One project, VentureStar, is planned as a replacement for the Space Shuttle and is designed to be a light single-stage launch vehicle. It would be a lot cheaper to run, costing one tenth of a Shuttle flight.

Mars Direct is a plan to send a robot factory to Mars to make fuel from Mars's atmosphere for a return journey. A second ship would follow later, carrying humans. They would use the fuel for a return flight to Earth.

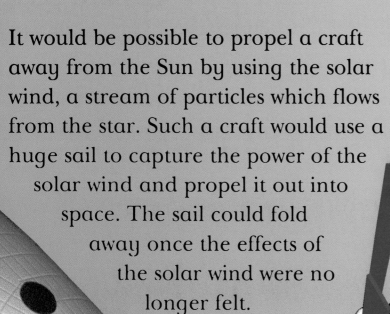

It would be possible to propel a craft away from the Sun by using the solar wind, a stream of particles which flows from the star. Such a craft would use a huge sail to capture the power of the solar wind and propel it out into space. The sail could fold away once the effects of the solar wind were no longer felt.

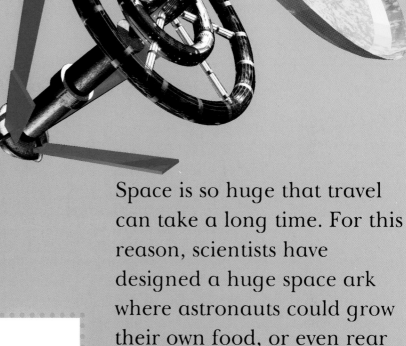

Space is so huge that travel can take a long time. For this reason, scientists have designed a huge space ark where astronauts could grow their own food, or even rear animals on a long journey.

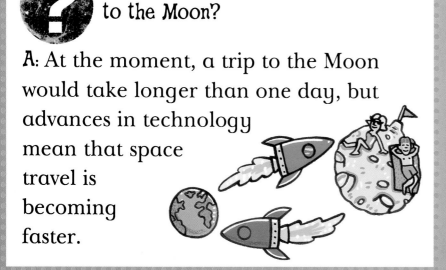

Q: Will there be day trips to the Moon?

A: At the moment, a trip to the Moon would take longer than one day, but advances in technology mean that space travel is becoming faster.

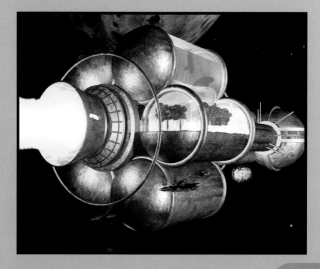

Chapter 4
The Universe

The Universe is very, very big—bigger than anything you can possibly imagine. It is not just all the stars, planets, and galaxies, but all the empty space in between as well. In fact, the Universe is everything that exists, from the tiniest atom to entire galaxies.

Which planet is named after the Roman goddess of love?*

Pluto

Uranus

Neptune

Saturn

Jupiter

Mars

Earth

Venus

Sun

Mercury

 Q: How big is our Solar System?

A: Our Solar System is so large it would take you over 5,000 years driving in a fast car to get to Pluto, the farthest planet from Earth!

*Venus

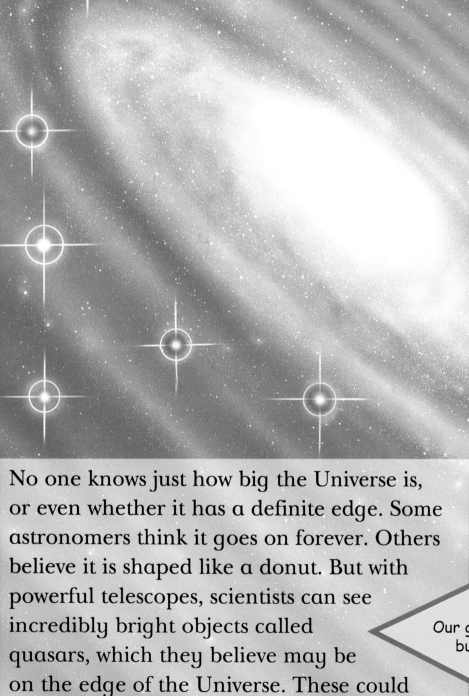

No one knows just how big the Universe is, or even whether it has a definite edge. Some astronomers think it goes on forever. Others believe it is shaped like a donut. But with powerful telescopes, scientists can see incredibly bright objects called quasars, which they believe may be on the edge of the Universe. These could be as far as 7 billion trillion miles away.

Awesome facts

Our galaxy, the Milky Way, seems huge, but the Universe contains at least 100 billion galaxies like ours!

The Big Bang

Scientists have worked out that the Universe began with an enormous explosion. One moment there was nothing, the next, there was a tiny, unbelievably hot, dense ball containing all the matter in the Universe. Then, a moment later, the Universe existed, blasting itself into life with the biggest explosion of all time—the Big Bang.

②

①

Q: How do we know about the Big Bang?

A: Every galaxy in the Universe is zooming away from ours. This shows the Universe is expanding. By plotting from the past how it has expanded, astronomers have worked out that the Universe began about 13 billion years ago.

1. No one knows quite why it all started. But scientists think it all began with a small, incredibly hot ball. In the first split second, it grew to the size of a basketball and then cooled down rapidly.

2. Gravity behaved very strangely. Instead of pulling things together, it blew them apart, and the Universe expanded at terrific speed. In a split second, it grew bigger than a galaxy.

3. As the Universe expanded, it cooled, and tiny particles of energy and matter began to appear. These particles formed a dense, immensely thick soup.

4. After about 3 minutes, gravity began to behave as it does now, drawing things together. Particles joined to make atoms, and atoms joined to make gases, such as hydrogen and helium.

5. Gases clumped into clouds. After several hundred million years, these clouds began to form stars and galaxies. These galaxies merged into clusters and superclusters, and much later the Sun and Solar System were formed. The Universe is still expanding and new planets and stars are still being formed.

Gravity

Every bit of matter in the Universe is pulled toward every other bit by an invisible force called gravity. It is what keeps you on the ground and holds the Solar System and the whole Universe together.

Earth's gravity pulls things to the ground—unless, like rockets, they use powerful engines to push in the opposite direction. Gravity also pulls the Moon into orbit around the Earth.

Exploring rocket

Jupiter is huge and is, in some ways, more like a star than a planet. Made mainly of hydrogen and helium, like the Sun, its strong gravity squeezes these gases until they are hot.

Rocket carrying satellite into orbit

Jet

The Sun's gravity keeps Earth in orbit around it.

Sun

Gravity is a mutual attraction between every bit of matter. A skydiver has a gravity that pulls, and he falls because he and the Earth pull each other together. But he falls to the Earth rather than Earth falling to him because the Earth is so much heavier and pulls so strongly.

Moon's orbit

Satellite's orbit

Earth's orbit

Q: How is gravity used to find out the size of stars?

A: The pull of gravity between two things like planets or stars depends on how massive they are, and how far apart they are. Astronomers can often tell how big a star is from how strongly its gravity appears to pull on nearby stars or planets.

Stars

Stars are the basic units of the Universe. There are nine planets in the Solar System that orbit our star, the Sun. However, astronomers have found at least 50 other planets in the Universe that circle other stars.

Awesome facts

There is a planet circling the distant star 51 Pegasi. Temperatures there are probably a scorching 2,400°F (1,315°C), and a year lasts just 4 days.

1

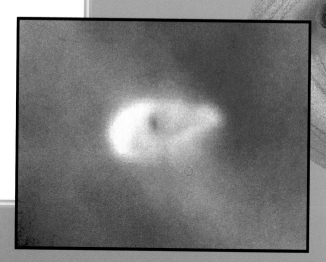

zoom in on...

New worlds

Even when they cannot see a new planet directly, astronomers may see a disk of matter around a star in which new planets are forming.

108

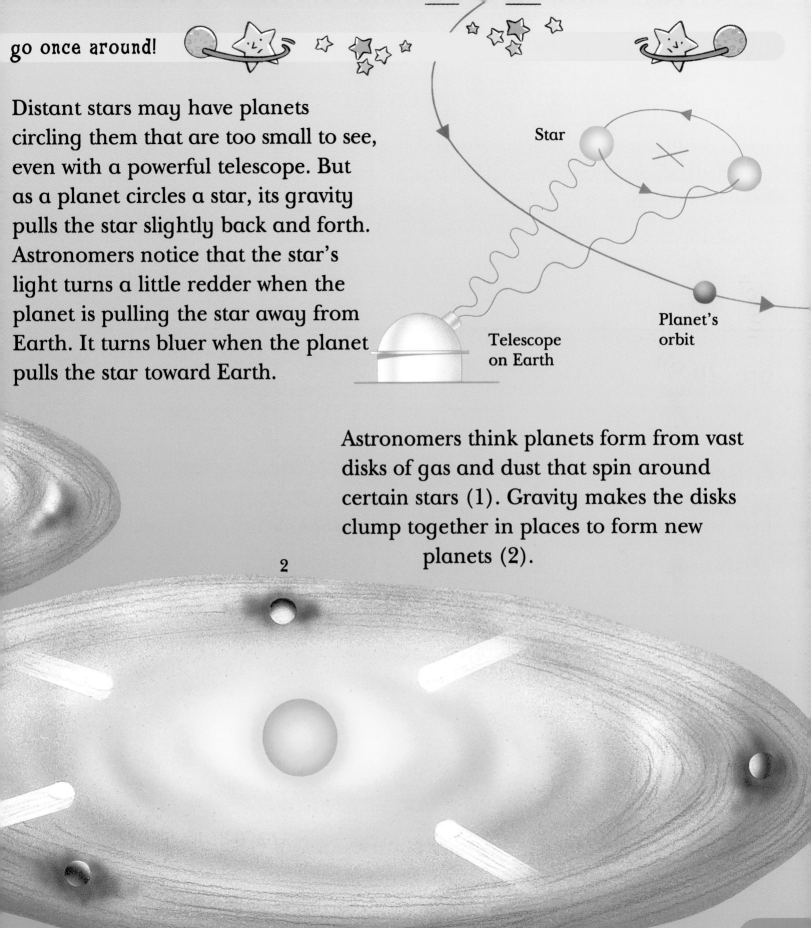

Distant stars may have planets circling them that are too small to see, even with a powerful telescope. But as a planet circles a star, its gravity pulls the star slightly back and forth. Astronomers notice that the star's light turns a little redder when the planet is pulling the star away from Earth. It turns bluer when the planet pulls the star toward Earth.

Star

Telescope on Earth

Planet's orbit

Astronomers think planets form from vast disks of gas and dust that spin around certain stars (1). Gravity makes the disks clump together in places to form new planets (2).

2

Awesome factS

The nearest star system, Alpha Centauri, is 4.2 light years away from Earth. This means that light would take 4.2 years to travel from this star to Earth.

Astronomers can tell from a star's color how fast it is moving. As it zooms away, the light waves get stretched out behind it. Stretched light waves look redder. The faster it is moving, the more the waves are stretched and the redder it looks.

The growing Universe

The Universe is incredibly big, and it is getting bigger! We know this because every galaxy we can see is rushing away from us. The farther away a galaxy is, the faster it is whizzing away.

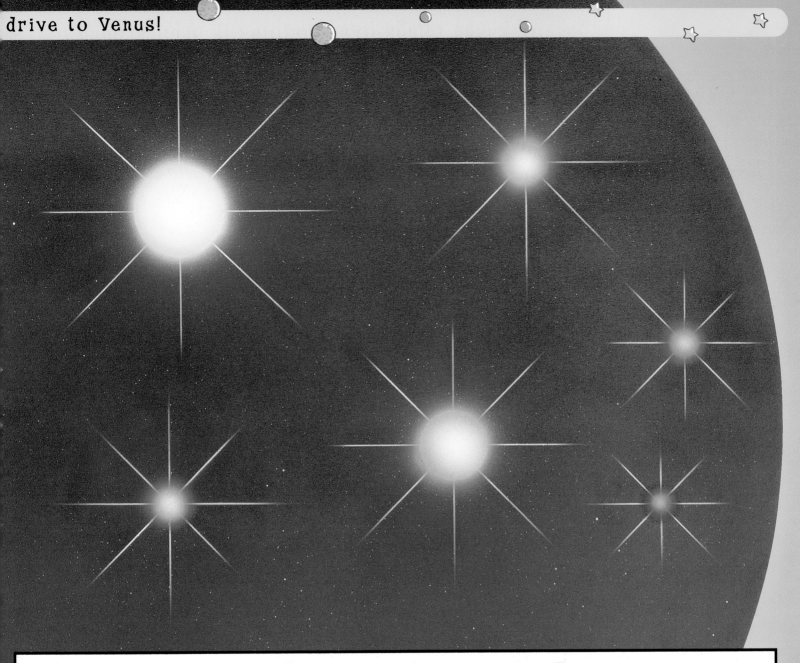

To see why galaxies move farther apart as the Universe expands, try this with a balloon. Stick paper stars on a partly inflated balloon to represent the galaxies. Then blow up the balloon more. You can see the stars (galaxies) moving farther apart as the balloon gets bigger.

Light and radiation

All the time, every second of the day and night, stars are beaming energy called radiation at us here on Earth. Some of this radiation, called visible light, is the light we can see. Most radiation, though, is invisible, coming in waves that our eyes cannot detect.

Our eyes can see only visible light. But astronomers have built special telescopes that pick up invisible radiation such as X-rays and radio waves. This means we can see much more of the stars and galaxies than our eyes alone show us. Indeed, stars such as Scorpius X-1 and Cygnus X-1 are known mainly by their X-ray and radio signals.

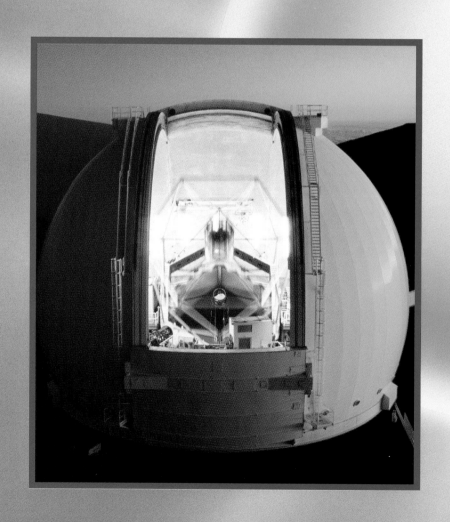

How light travels

We know that light and other kinds of radiation travel in a straight line, faster than anything else in the Universe. But scientists were long unsure whether light moved like waves in the sea or like a bouncing ball. They now believe it is a combination of both—minute packets of vibrating energy called photons.

Awesome facts

Astronomers' telescopes can register light sent out by distant stars billions of years ago. This light can help us discover the history of the Universe.

Star clusters

Stars are not spread evenly across space. Instead, they huddle together in clumps called clusters, attracted by their own mutual gravity. New clusters are forming all the time, but some are billions of years old.

With the Hubble Space Telescope, astronomers found that clusters contain more stars than were visible before. Hubble showed that this cluster, NGC 1850 (right), thought to contain only about 1,000 stars, actually contains at least 10,000 stars.

What is the other name for the Pleiades?

zoom in on...

Pleiades

The newest clusters, called open clusters, contain several hundred stars. The Pleiades, or Seven Sisters, is an open cluster in the constellation of Taurus. Some of its individual stars can be seen with the naked eye, but it also contains hundreds of stars too faint to see.

Globular clusters

Around the edge of our galaxy, there are about 140 large, old clusters called globular clusters (left). There are often 100,000 stars in a globular cluster, and sometimes up to a million. As the galaxy spins around, so do these clusters, taking about 100 million years to go around the galaxy once.

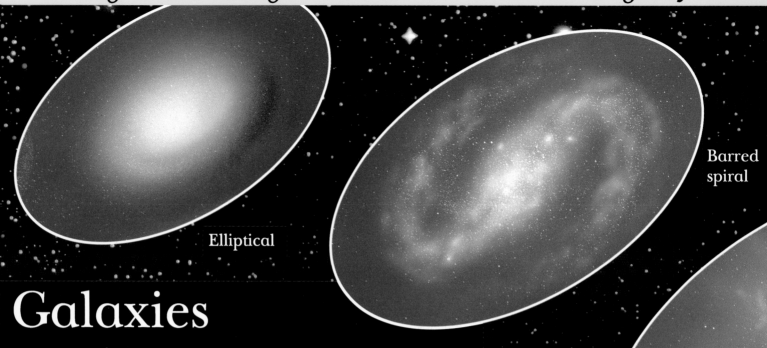

Elliptical

Barred
spiral

Galaxies

Just as stars are gathered in clusters, so clusters of stars are clumped into vast star cities called galaxies. The biggest galaxies are incredibly large and can contain thousands of billions of stars.

Galaxies zoom around in all directions. Every now and then they crash into each other. Irregular galaxies like the Small Magellanic Cloud may be the debris from such a galactic pileup.

Q: How old are galaxies?

A: Scientists cannot agree how old galaxies are. Most believe that many elliptical galaxies date back almost to the dawn of time and are at least ten billion years old!

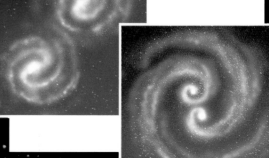

Most galaxies are spiral in shape. A quarter of all galaxies are "irregular." Some galaxies are barred spirals. The biggest galaxies are round or fried-egg-shaped "elliptical" galaxies.

Irregular

The Andromeda galaxy is the nearest to the Milky Way. It is still so far away that without a telescope it just looks like a faint blur. Over two million light years away, it is the farthest thing we can see with the naked eye.

Spiral

117

The Milky Way

Our Sun is just one of 100 billion stars grouped together in a galaxy called the Milky Way. The Milky Way is often called the Galaxy, but is actually just one of more than 30 billion spiral galaxies in the Universe.

Spot the group of stars represented by a dog.

Canis Major

Puppis

Vela

Carina

Centaurus

Crux

Muca

Triangulum Australe

Ara

Our Sun, with its Solar System of planets, is just one of millions of stars on one of the arms of the Milky Way. The whole galaxy sweeps the Sun around at about 62 million miles (100m km) per hour! The Sun goes once around the galaxy in just 225 million years.

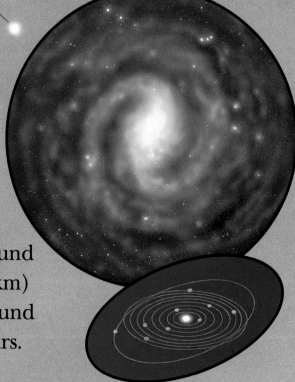

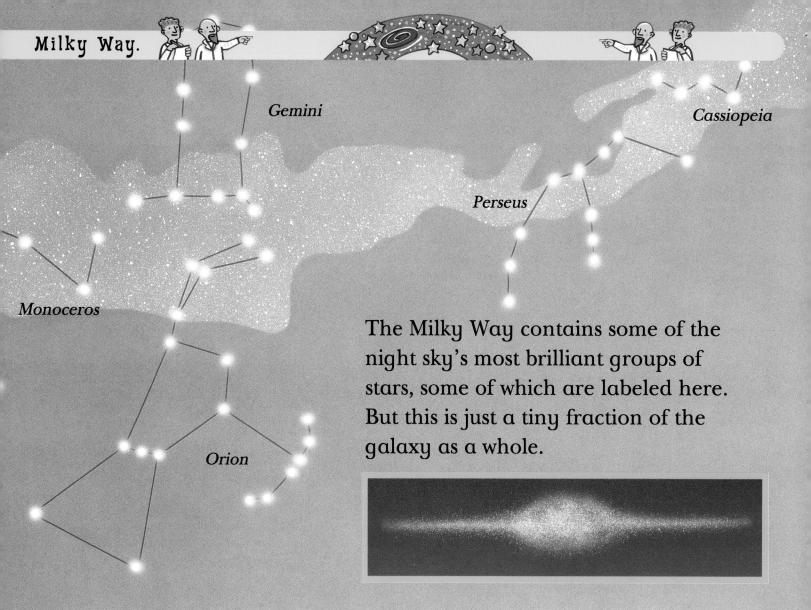

Gemini

Cassiopeia

Perseus

Monoceros

Orion

The Milky Way contains some of the night sky's most brilliant groups of stars, some of which are labeled here. But this is just a tiny fraction of the galaxy as a whole.

Q: Why is it called the Milky Way?

A: If you're far from town on a dark, clear night, you can see a hazy band of light stretching across the sky. You are actually seeing an edge-on view of part of the Milky Way galaxy with its countless stars. People long ago called it the Milky Way because it looked like someone had spilled milk across the sky.

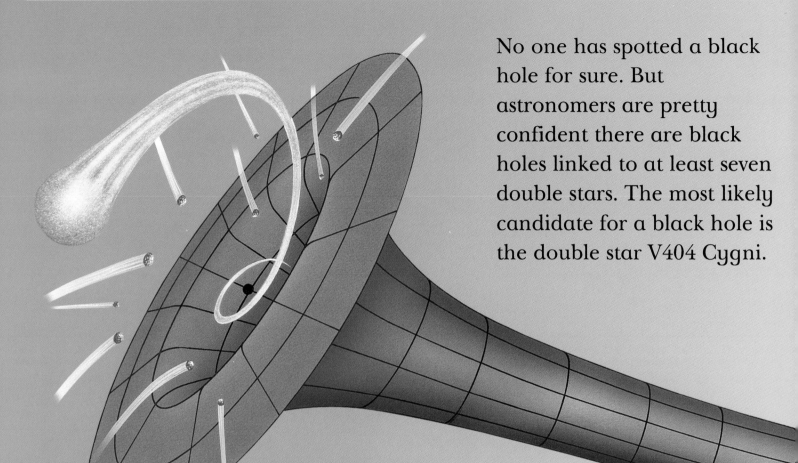

No one has spotted a black hole for sure. But astronomers are pretty confident there are black holes linked to at least seven double stars. The most likely candidate for a black hole is the double star V404 Cygni.

This picture shows a black hole as a funnel because matter, radiation, and even space and time are sucked into a black hole like water down a drain. In fact, a black hole is small and round, and its surface is called an event horizon. If you go beyond the event horizon, you go out of space and time into nothingness.

Enormous black holes may be at the heart of every galaxy, including the Milky Way. These black holes may contain as much matter as millions of Suns, in a space no bigger than the Solar System.

Black holes

Black holes are points in space where gravity is so strong that it sucks in everything. These points even suck in light, so they can't be seen. This is why they are called "black" holes.

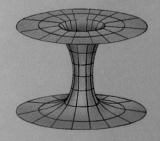
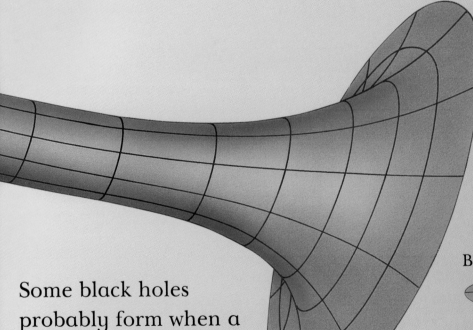

Some scientists think there are white holes, too. If black holes are like drains sucking in everything, then white holes are fountains, where it all gushes out again. If we could join a black hole to a white hole, perhaps we could create a tunnel, a short cut, through space.

Some black holes probably form when a huge star burns out. It is squeezed so tightly by its own gravity that all of its matter is crushed into a tiny point before it vanishes completely.

Black hole

White hole

Black hole and white hole join, forming tunnel

Black hole and white hole separate
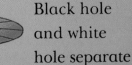

Active galaxies

We see many galaxies because they beam out visible light. But there are some that beam out powerful surges of X-rays, radio waves, and other invisible forms of radiation. Astronomers call these galaxies active galaxies.

When astronomers look at the galaxy Centaurus-A using X-rays, they see a band of bright spots on either side of the galaxy's core. They believe these bright spots are gas particles, shot out of the core of a black hole, surging through the galaxy's magnetic field.

The jets sent out by the black hole at the core of the Centaurus-A galaxy generate X-rays and radio waves. They beam out radio signals that make the most powerful radio beacon on Earth seem very weak by comparison. The gas jets are 100 times larger than our entire galaxy.

An active galaxy beams out awesome amounts of energy. Astronomers think the source of all this power is a massive black hole that is sucking in entire stars. As the black hole shreds a star, it spews out jets of gas that generate X-rays and radio waves.

A photo of the galaxy Centaurus-A (above) shows a different view from the X-ray photo (left). The galaxy's core is believed to be a massive disk of gas spinning around a huge black hole.

Superclusters are grouped in loops and superwalls, separated by voids 400 million light years across.

Superclusters

Cluster of galaxies

Super-structures

Just as clusters of stars form galaxies, so galaxies group to form even larger structures. Our Milky Way galaxy is over 100,000 light years across, but it is just part of a group of 40 galaxies called the Local Group.

Just as galaxies form the Local Group, so the Local Group is clumped with other groups of galaxies to form clusters of thousands of galaxies. Half a dozen or so clusters are, in turn, grouped into large superclusters 200 million light years across.

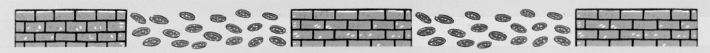

zoom in on...

Great Wall

The biggest known structure in the Universe is the Great Wall. It is a superwall, a group of superclusters, some 500 million light years across. But even this may not be the biggest structure. There may even be structures three billion light years across!

Local group

Milky Way

Great Wall of galaxies

The Big Crunch

Scientists are looking into the sky for clues about the fate of the Universe. Will it go on growing forever—the open Universe? Will it stop growing and just stay the same size—steady state? Or will it eventually shrink again—the Big Crunch?

Big Bang

Q: What is the Big Crunch?
A: If there is a lot of invisible matter in the Universe, its gravity will pull the Universe back together again. The Universe will start to shrink, until it all ends up the size of a marble—the Big Crunch.

Awesome factS
Current theories suggest our Universe may be just one of many in existence. Lots of Universes may be bubbling up all the time beyond space and time.

1. Continual expansion

2. Universe remains steady

3. Big Crunch

The fate of the Universe probably depends on how much invisible matter there is to hold it together. If there is too little, the Universe will go on getting gradually bigger (1), if there is more, it will remain steady (2), if there is more still, it will all end in the Big Crunch (3).

Constellations

People have always made up stories about the stars, linking them into groups and naming them after characters. These groups are called constellations. Astronomers recognize 88 in all. You can use these constellations to divide the sky and find your way around from star to star.

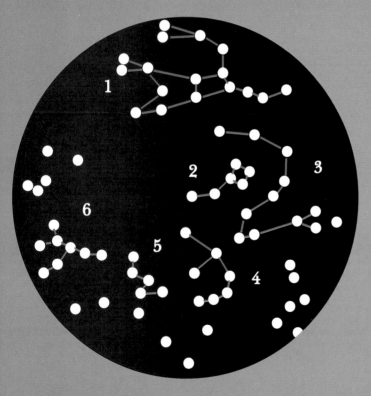

1. Ursa Major
2. Ursa Minor
3. Draco
4. Cepheus
5. Cassiopeia
6. Perseus

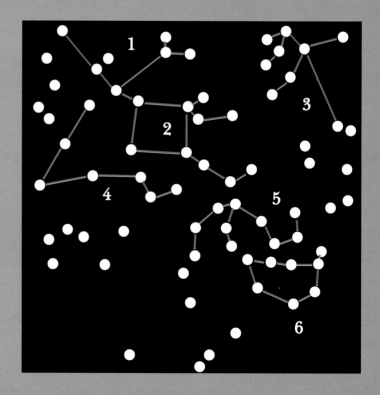

1. Andromeda
2. Pegasus
3. Cygnus
4. Aquarius
5. Capricornus
6. Pisces

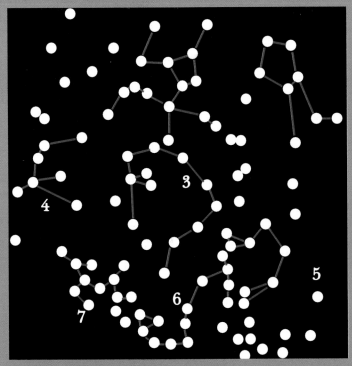

1. Hercules   5. Libra
2. Boötes   6. Scorpius
3. Ophiucus   7. Sagittarius
4. Aquila

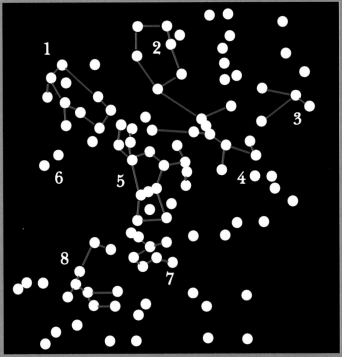

1. Gemini   5. Orion
2. Auriga   6. Canis Minor
3. Aries   7. Lepus
4. Taurus   8. Canis Major

1. Leo   4. Corvus
2. Cancer   5. Virgo
3. Hydra

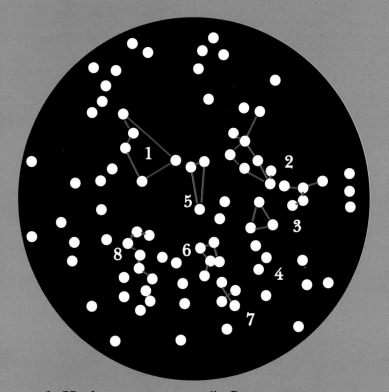

1. Hydrus   5. Octans
2. Pavo   6. Musca
3. Ara   7. Crux
4. Triangulum   8. Volans
    Australe

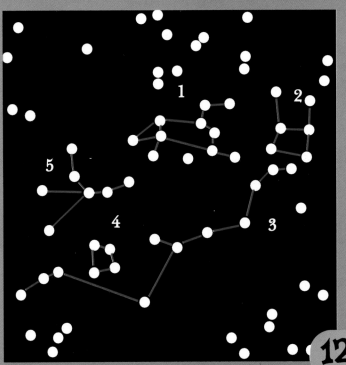

Star charts

These charts show the constellations that you can see in the night sky at different times of year.

The map below shows the northern hemisphere sky, the map on the right shows the southern hemisphere sky.

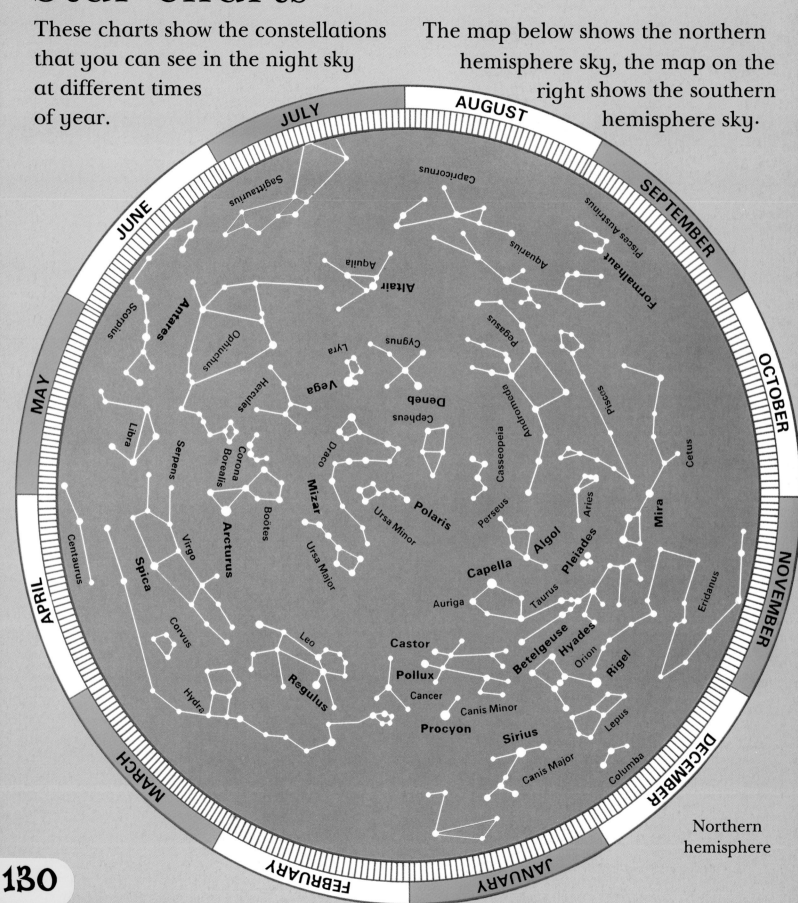

Northern hemisphere

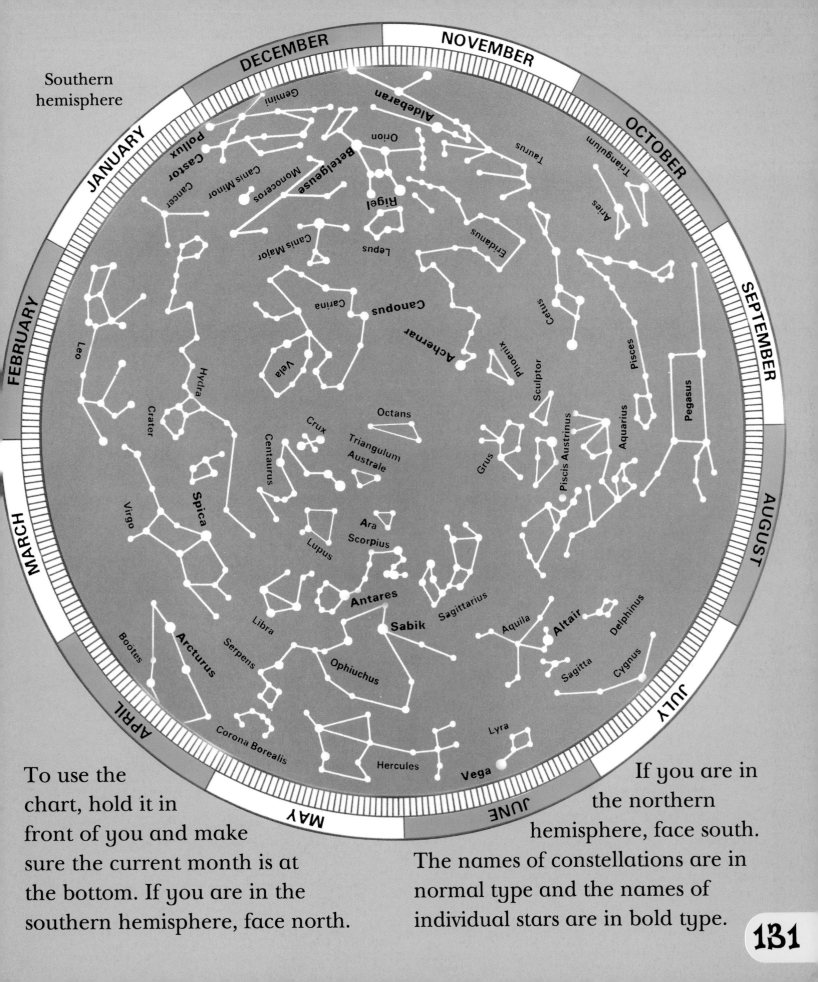

Southern hemisphere

DECEMBER
NOVEMBER
OCTOBER
SEPTEMBER
AUGUST
JULY
JUNE
MAY
APRIL
MARCH
FEBRUARY
JANUARY

Gemini
Pollux
Castor
Cancer
Canis Minor
Monoceros
Canis Major
Hydra
Crater
Leo
Virgo
Spica
Centaurus
Vela
Carina
Canopus
Betelgeuse
Rigel
Orion
Lepus
Aldebaran
Taurus
Eridanus
Triangulum
Aries
Cetus
Pisces
Pegasus
Aquarius
Sculptor
Phoenix
Achernar
Octans
Crux
Triangulum Australe
Ara
Scorpius
Lupus
Libra
Antares
Sabik
Sagittarius
Grus
Piscis Austrinus
Aquila
Altair
Delphinus
Sagitta
Cygnus
Lyra
Vega
Hercules
Ophiuchus
Corona Borealis
Serpens
Arcturus
Boötes

To use the chart, hold it in front of you and make sure the current month is at the bottom. If you are in the southern hemisphere, face north.

If you are in the northern hemisphere, face south. The names of constellations are in normal type and the names of individual stars are in bold type.

131

Planet facts

Here are some facts about the
planets that you may like to know.

MERCURY
36
88 days
59 days
3,029
0

VENUS
67
225 days
243 days
7,521
0

JUPITER
483
12 years
10 hours
88,846
16

EARTH
93
365 1/4 days
23 hours 56 mins
7,926
1

MARS
142
687 days
24 1/2 hours
4,213
2

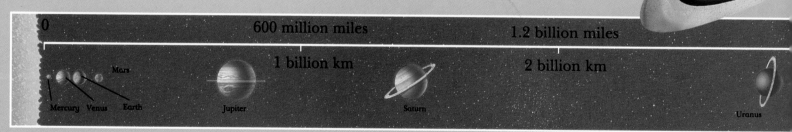

0   600 million miles   1.2 billion miles

1 billion km   2 billion km

Mars

Mercury   Venus   Earth   Jupiter   Saturn   Uranus

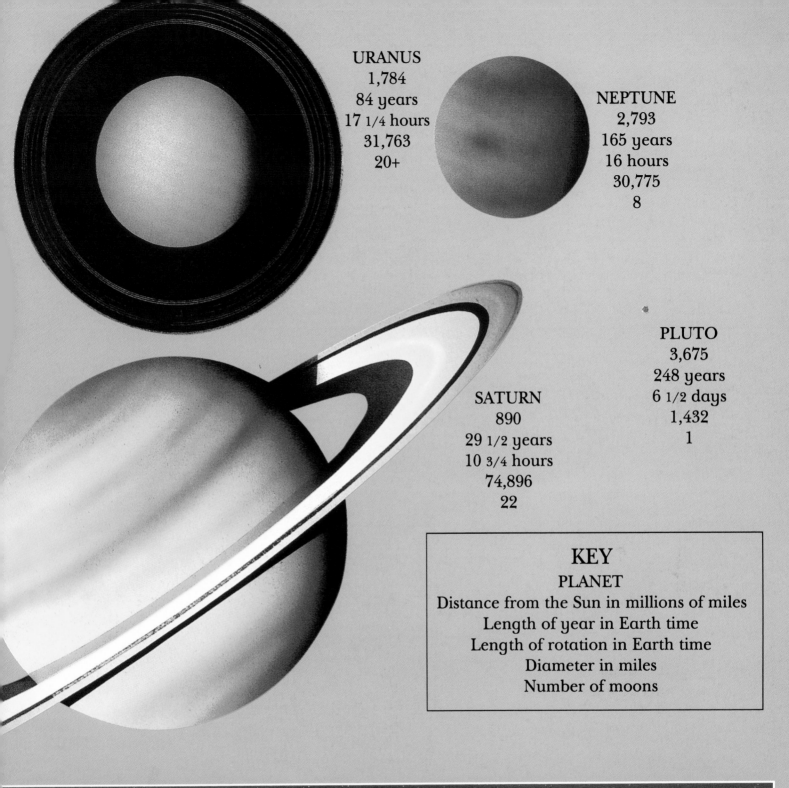

URANUS
1,784
84 years
17 1/4 hours
31,763
20+

NEPTUNE
2,793
165 years
16 hours
30,775
8

PLUTO
3,675
248 years
6 1/2 days
1,432
1

SATURN
890
29 1/2 years
10 3/4 hours
74,896
22

KEY
PLANET
Distance from the Sun in millions of miles
Length of year in Earth time
Length of rotation in Earth time
Diameter in miles
Number of moons

2 billion miles   2½ billion miles   3 billion miles   3½ billion miles

3 billion km   4 billion km   5 billion km   6 billion km

Neptune

Pluto

Space missions

There have been so many missions into space that it is difficult to remember all of them. However, here are some of the most recent missions and even some more planned for the future!

Mars Surveyor

The Mars Global Surveyor reached Mars in September 1997. Its mission is to accurately map the planet's entire surface. From its orbit around Mars, its cameras can see objects that are less than 3 feet (1 m) across.

IRAS

The IRAS satellite was designed to pick up radiation given out by anything hot. IRAS turned gradually around to map a picture of the entire sky. It picked up asteroids, comet dust trails, and gas and dust where stars were being born.

Cassini
Cassini will reach Saturn in 2004 and will spend four years in orbit looking at the planet. It also carries a small probe called Huygens, which it will drop onto Saturn's moon, Titan.

Mars Direct
A mission to Mars would cost billions of dollars, so scientists have planned a cheaper alternative. Using Mars Direct, a robot factory would be sent to Mars where it would create fuel from Mars's atmosphere. After a year, a second ship would carry a human crew to Mars without all the fuel. This method would cut the cost of any Mars mission.

Darwin Space Telescope
In the near future, scientists are hoping to launch an amazing multiple space telescope called Darwin. It is not just one telescope but six, which will float in space linked to a central unit by lasers. It will orbit the Sun between Mars and Jupiter.

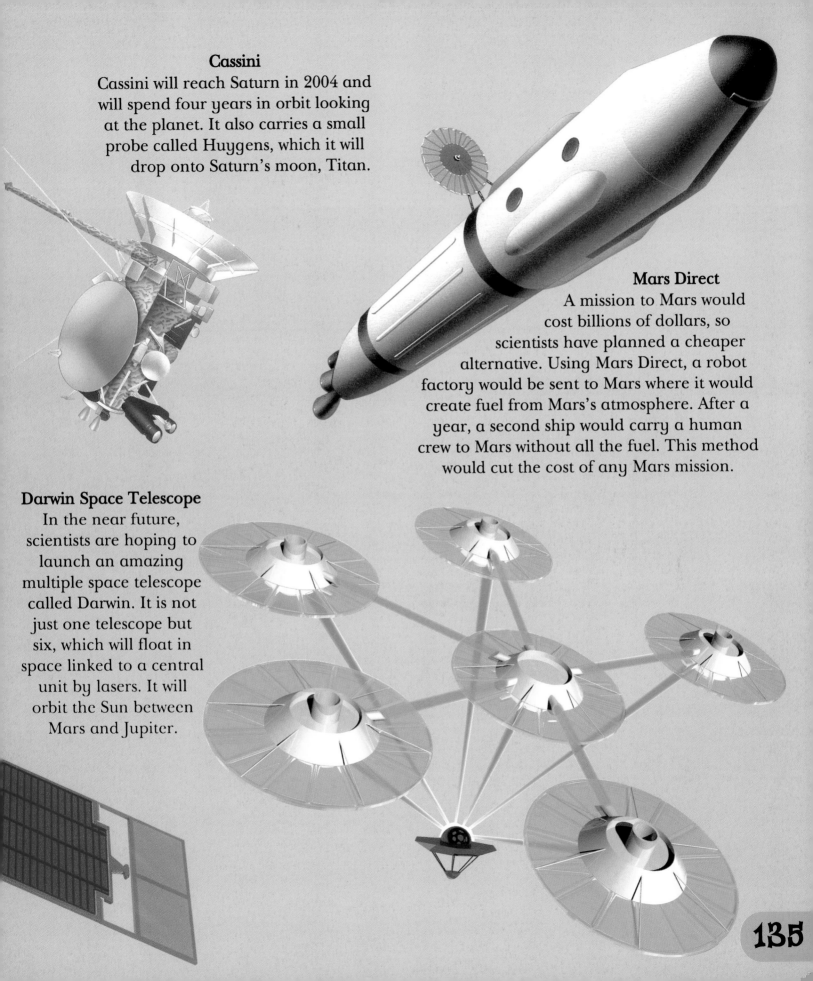

Universe facts

The Universe is enormous, and it can be difficult to understand its size. Below is an illustration that will help to give you some idea of the proportions of the Universe!

Our Solar System
13 light hours across

Sun
our star,
8 light minutes
from Earth

Earth

Moon
1 light second
from Earth

Milky Way
100,000 light
years across

Andromeda
our nearest galaxy,
2.6 million light years
from Earth

Pluto
the farthest
planet, 5.5 light
hours from Earth

Alpha Centauri
our nearest star system,
4.2 light years
from Earth

Glossary

Active galaxy
A galaxy that emits huge amounts of radiation including radio waves and X-rays. Astronomers believe that active galaxies have a black hole at their center.

Asteroids
Small, rocky objects, the greatest collection of which orbit the Sun in a band called the asteroid belt, between Mars and Jupiter.

Astronauts
People who travel into space. Russian astronauts are called cosmonauts.

Atmosphere
The layer of gases that surrounds a planet. The atmosphere around the Earth supplies us with the oxygen that keeps us alive.

Aurora
A bright and colorful glow in the Earth's atmosphere which occurs when particles from the Sun, called the solar wind, enter the atmosphere, usually at the poles.

Big Bang
A huge explosion about 13 billion years ago that many astronomers believe started the Universe.

Big Crunch
A possible end to the Universe. This could occur if all the matter in the Universe is pulled together by gravity, ending in a Big Crunch.

Black hole
The remains of a huge star that has exploded and collapsed in on itself. The gravity is so strong that not even light can escape.

Comets
Lumps of ice and dust that orbit the Sun. As a comet approaches the Sun, heat from the Sun causes the ice and dust to boil off, creating huge tails that stretch out behind the comet.

Constellation
A group of stars in the night sky. Astronomers recognize 88 of them.

Core
The central part of an object. The Earth's core is made of metal; a comet's core is made up of rock and ice.

Corona
The outer atmosphere of the Sun. It can be seen during a solar eclipse.

Crater

A bowl-shaped pit on the surface of a planet. Some are caused by volcanoes, and some by the impact of a meteorite.

Eclipse

When one planet or star passes in front of another. A solar eclipse occurs when the Moon lies between the Earth and the Sun, and a lunar ecplise occurs when the Earth lies between the Sun and the Moon.

Equator

An imaginary line that runs around the middle of a planet at an equal distance from its two poles.

Escape velocity

The speed at which a rocket has to travel in order to escape from the pull of the Earth's gravity. Escape velocity is 25,000 miles (40,000 km) per hour.

Extraterrestrial

Any object that comes from anywhere outside planet Earth.

Galaxy

An enormous cluster of stars. Each galaxy can contain many billions of stars. Galaxies can be spiral, barred spiral, elliptical, or irregular.

Gas giant

A large planet made mainly of hydrogen. Jupiter, Saturn, Uranus, and Neptune are all gas giants.

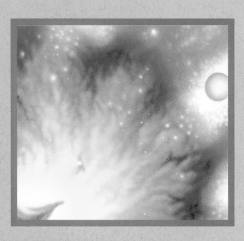

Gravity

Every object in the Universe has a force that attracts it to every other object. This force is called gravity. The Solar System is held together by the Sun's gravitational pull.

Great Red Spot

A dark red swirl of clouds in Jupiter's atmosphere.

Light year

A unit used to measure distance in space. It is the distance light travels in one year, that is about 6 trillion (9.5 trillion km).

Magnetic field

A region in space where a magnetic force is in operation.

Matter

Any material that exists and takes up space.

Meteorite

A meteoroid that hits the Earth's surface.

Meteoroids

Small pieces of space debris that orbit the Sun.

Meteors

Objects that hit the Earth's atmosphere and burn up, leaving a fiery tail that disappears after a few seconds.

Milky Way

The galaxy in which our Solar System is situated.

Glossary

Moons
Small bodies that orbit some of the major planets. Earth has one moon, Venus has none, and Jupiter has 16.

Nebula
A cloud of gas and dust, where stars are born.

Neutron star
The remains of a star that has exploded in a supernova.

Nuclear fusion
The process by which atoms are squeezed together until they combine, releasing huge amounts of energy. Fusion occurs inside stars, causing them to shine.

Observatory
A building that houses a telescope.

Orbit
The path of an object, such as a planet or a comet, around another object, such as a star.

Orbiter
An artificial satellite after the launch rockets and boosters have fallen away.

Photon
A tiny packet of vibrating energy.

Planets
Large objects that orbit a star. These can be rocky planets such as the Earth, Venus, or Mars, or gassy giant planets, such as Jupiter, Saturn, or Uranus.

Pole
A point on a planet's surface around which the planet spins or rotates.

Probe
An unmanned spacecraft sent from Earth to explore an object in space.

Pulsar
A neutron star that emits energy as it spins.

Quasar
An object in space that emits an enormous amount of energy. Quasars are thought to be at the center of very distant galaxies.

Radiation
Energy that can be visible light, or waves that our eyes cannot see, such as X-rays or radio waves.

Rings

The larger, gassy planets—Jupiter, Saturn, Uranus, and Neptune—are surrounded by rings. These rings are not

solid as they appear from a distance. They are actually made up of particles of rock and ice.

Rockets

Powerful motors that produce thrust to blast off into space.

Satellite

An object that orbits another larger object. Satellites can be natural, such as moons, or artificial, such as a spacecraft.

Solar panels

Panels on a spacecraft that convert the Sun's light into energy for power.

Solar System

The group of major planets, including Earth, and minor planets that orbit the Sun.

Solar wind

A stream of particles that flows from the Sun.

Space

Everything above the Earth's atmosphere.

Stages

Rockets may come in parts, called stages. Each stage contains its own rocket motors and fuel.

Star

A large ball of gas in the Universe that produces light and heat.

Sunspots

Patches on the Sun's surface that are darker than the surrounding area. They appear darker because they

are not as hot as the gas around them.

Supernova

When a massive star runs out of fuel, it explodes. The enormous explosion is called a supernova.

Telescope

An instrument that collects light and radiation, and magnifies them to help astronomers study the sky.

Universe

Everything that exists, from the tiniest atoms to entire galaxies and beyond.

Void

An empty space or area.

White dwarf

A small star at the end of its life. It is the core of a red giant star.

X-rays

Radiation that cannot be seen with the naked eye.

Year

The time it takes a planet to orbit a star. The Earth takes 365 $\frac{1}{4}$ days.

Index

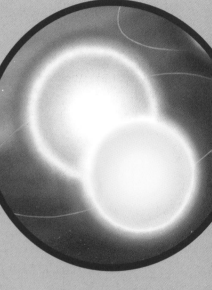

143

Index

Photocredits
t-top, b-bottom, l-left, r-right,
c-center, m-main.
All photographs supplied by Corbis
except for:
Back cover mr, 6-7, 11br, 12-13 all,
20tl, 24mr, 44-45, 46-47, 50, 51ml,
52tr both, 65mr, 80bl, 83tr, 93bl, 94br
both, 97tl, 140mt—Stockbyte. 4tl, 16-
17, 22br, 78tr, 88bl, 98-99, 112, 115tr,
144c—Roger Ressmeyer/Corbis. 30
—Robin Scagell/Galaxy. 32 all, 114,
138tr—STScl/Galaxy. 79—B. Cooper
& D. Parker/Science Photo Library.
82m—Bettman/Corbis. 82ml, 90-91,
115ml—CORBIS. 94tl, 100-101, 108br
—NASA. 107mr, 138tl—Alistair
Wright; The Military Picture
Library/CORBIS. 117tr—Michael
Stecker/Galaxy. 122—Dr. Eric
Feigelson/Science Photo Library.